A Primer on Corporate Governance

A Primer on Corporate Governance

Mexico

Jose Luis Rivas

BEP BUSINESS EXPERT PRESS

First published in 2020 by
Business Expert Press, LLC
222 East 46th Street, New York, NY 10017
www.businessexpertpress.com

ISBN-13: 978-1-63157-581-5 (paperback)
ISBN-13: 978-1-63157-582-2 (e-book)

Business Expert Press Corporate Governance Collection

Collection ISSN: 1948-0470 (print)
Collection ISSN: 1948-0415 (electronic)

Cover image by Pressmaster/Shutterstock.com
Cover and interior design by S4Carlisle Publishing Services Private Ltd.,
Chennai, India

First edition: 2020

10 9 8 7 6 5 4 3 2 1

Printed in the United States of America.

Dedication

To my father who showed me the value of persistence…

Abstract

Mexico is a land inhabited by several indigenous civilizations and was conquered by Spain in 1521. The country is mostly a racial mix between the Spanish and native cultures. It is a traditionalist society where family, religion, and culture play a key role. The role of the marketplace is constrained by the government and local interest groups such as unions, political parties, commerce chambers, and private firms. The market for corporate control is scarce. Corporate governance codes are voluntary.

Corporate ownership is concentrated with few institutional investors. Shareholder activism is uncommon. Corporate boards are single tier in nature. CEO duality is common practice. Boards are made mostly of insiders and shareholder representatives. Independent board members hold minority stakes.

This book starts by describing the macro context in which Mexico is embedded. We then focus on its corporate governance system: laws, regulatory bodies, code of good governance, stock market and the peculiarities of local business groups. The central part of the book summarizes key characteristics of board structure and networks in the country. The book ends with interviews of two well-known directors and suggestions to move the governance field forward in Mexico.

Keywords

Corporate governance; boards; Mexico; emerging country; institutions; business groups; family business; ownership structure; Latin America

Contents

Foreword

Jose Luis Rivas's book on Mexican corporate governance represents an outstanding contribution to knowledge about corporate governance not only in Mexico, but also in developing countries more generally. This book represents an excellent starting place for anyone interested in researching corporate governance in contexts outside the United States or the United Kingdom. Most research on corporate governance is dominated by theory and evidence from the two large developed countries, and our understanding of corporate governance more generally is perhaps harmed by an overreliance on these two countries. Jose's book starts with a deep understanding that context matters in corporate governance, and that context involves institutions that extend to political and legal systems as well as social and cultural mores.

Starting from the perspective that institutions are critical to good corporate governance, the book describes the state of many of the institutions that are relevant to governance in Mexico. Factors that make Mexican corporate governance substantially different from that in the United States and the United Kingdom are highlighted. Factors like expropriation of investor wealth by controlling shareholders, challenges in setting up businesses in Mexico, difficulties in contract enforcement and the seeking of legal remedies, and the very dominant role that families and political influence have on publicly traded corporations in Mexico are all described both qualitatively and with statistical evidence.

The author is well steeped in the Mexican context. He was born and raised in Mexico, and aside for a few brief stints (MBA at Northwestern, a PhD at IE Business School, and a year-long visit to Arizona State University), he has spent his life there. At the same time, he is a close observer of corporate governance in the US context and has ongoing research projects focused on the United States as well as Latin America.

One of the great gems in the book is Jose's interview with Jaime Serra-Puche—an executive with wide experience as a director in both Mexican and US firms. The interview highlights in rather stark terms the differences in how boards function in Mexico relative to the United States. It also illustrates how deeply culturally embedded the corporate governance differences are, highlighting the challenges for policy makers who want to make corporate governance in Mexico more efficient and effective. The interview is brief, but the subject is honest and forthright about his own experiences and observations, and the reader walks away with a much deeper understanding of the issues at hand.

The book also provides an absolute wealth of hand-collected data, conveyed through figures and tables. All of this data is used to both illustrate assertions made by the author and provide empirical evidence to support the conclusions drawn by the author. Importantly, the data can also be used by readers not only for quick tests of intuitive predictions, but also as a starting point for much deeper and richer data collection efforts. Jose's suggestions for issues to study moving forward serve as a good guide for those interested in taking the next steps to better understand corporate governance in developing countries.

Albert Cannella, Jr.
Endowed Chair
Texas A&M University

Acknowledgments

I would like to thank the editor of the corporate governance series, Jack Pearce, who guided me through the complicated path of improving this book. To Bert Canella for the continuous support of this project. Special thanks also to Guillermo de Alva and Eliel Garcia Soto for their help with data collection. Finally, I would like to thank Bill Judge, who introduced me to Rob Zwettler and the BEP team.

The completion of this book was partially supported by Asociación Mexicana de Cultura AC.

Introduction

The corporate governance scandals in the United States and Europe as well as the financial crises of 2008 to 2009 have made corporate governance (CG) a widely debated topic. A significant number of countries have revised their CG codes and regulations in order to increase the levels of CG efficacy.

This book is about corporate governance in Mexico. It is intended to provide an understanding of the characteristics and peculiarities of corporate governance of large Mexican firms. We have attempted to build on knowledge accumulated in the academic and professional empirical research. Our approach has the advantage of being grounded in factual evidence rather than being merely based on opinion. Hence, we believe this book can provide insights for practitioners and academics to make better judgments when confronted with CG issues in Mexico.

The book is divided in six parts. Part 1 looks at corporate governance from a macro perspective. It starts by explaining the peculiarities of corporate governance in emerging countries. It also summarizes the main contextual issues in Mexico and ends with a CG score comparison of Mexico and its main trading partners: the United States, Canada, Spain, South Korea, China, and the United Kingdom.

Part 2 of the book focuses on the Mexican CG system: its laws and regulatory bodies, the Mexican code of good governance, the historical evolution of the stock market and the peculiarities of local business groups that have been part of its corporate history since the 19th century. We finish part 2 by summarizing findings of the most recent academic articles (1998 to 2018) dealing with CG in Mexico.

Part 3 introduces the reader to a central piece of the Mexican governance equation: families. Because a significant majority of the largest firms are owned by families, we thought it would be worthwhile to review how different types of family involvement—*ownership, management, and boards*—might have different consequences for firm performance.

Part 4 is a central part of this book since it summarizes key characteristics of board structure and networks in the country.

Part 5 presents interviews with two of the most central directors in Mexico: Jaime Serra-Puche and Claudio X Gonzalez. Jaime is a leading independent director who was the chief negotiator of the North American Free Trade Agreement (NAFTA). Don Claudio is chairman of Kimberly Clark Mexico and former president of the Mexican Business Roundtable (CMN-Consejo Mexicano de Negocios).

Finally, part 6 presents suggestions to move the field forward in Mexico.

CHAPTER 1

The Emerging Market Context: Why Does It Matter?

Corporate governance is the "set of mechanisms used to manage the relationship among stakeholders that is used to determine and control the strategic direction and performance of organizations" (Lynall, Golden, and Hillman 2003). Corporate governance helps ensure that a firm's strategic decisions are made effectively and in line with shareholders' interests. It aligns owners' and managers' decisions. It is also a reflection of the firm's values and beliefs. Efficient corporate governance mechanisms can be a competitive advantage for a firm.

Until recently, the need for corporate governance laid on the idea that when separation exists between firm ownership and its management, self-interested managers can take actions to benefit themselves, with firm stakeholders bearing the cost for this action. This scenario is typically referred to as the agency problem. Costs associated with the agency problem can include:

A) Financial restatement
B) Fraud related to bankruptcies
C) Stock option backdating
D) Earnings manipulation

Corporate governance is then implemented to decrease the risk of incurring agency costs.

According to a McKinsey study (Newell and Wilson 2002), institutional investors are willing to pay premiums for well-governed firms.

Premiums go from a low of 11 percent in Canada to a high of 40 percent in Egypt. Foreigners invest less money in firms that insiders control and that are domiciled in countries with weak investor protection (Leuz, Lins, and Warnock 2009). Because institutional weakness makes law enforcement costly and more difficult to achieve, the quality of country-level institutions influences corporate governance at the firm level. High ownership concentration is a response to the lack of legal protection.

Weak corporate governance, ownership concentration, and limited protection of investors—*all of them emerging market characteristics*—intensify principal–agent problems and create unique agency problems where majority owners take advantage of minority ones. This has been labeled the "principal–principal" problem (Young et al. 2008).

In emerging countries, laws and regulations on accounting requirements, information transparency, and stock market transactions are absent or deficient. Hence, standard structures of corporate governance have little institutional support. Therefore, diversified business groups, family connections, and government contacts play a larger role in a firm's governance activities and conflicts between majority and minority shareholders are the norm.

The expropriation from minority shareholders can take place in several ways:

A) Designating nonqualified individuals to key corporate roles.
B) Buying and selling at nonmarket prices from organizations related to majority shareholders.
C) Pursuing strategies that advance personal, family, or political agendas in detriment of firm performance objectives.

Hostile takeovers or a market for corporate control is the ultimate solution for this problem, but this mechanism does not exist in most emerging countries.

Institutional weakness also inhibits majority owners from sharing sensitive information with potential investors; building trust is difficult and this probably inclines controlling shareholders to prefer loyalty over aptitude when choosing among potential directors and top managers. A negative family dynamic in a context of low legal protection will probably increase the risk of expropriation for minority shareholders even if they are members of the founding family (González et al. 2015).

Research evidence has shown that principal–principal problems in emerging countries can be decreased by having multiple block holders (i.e., banks or private equity funds) that help monitor the firm and stronger legal institutions. On the other hand, expropriation of minority shareholders tends to increase with a family chief executive officer (CEO) and the political involvement of owners (Azoury and Bouri 2015; Jiang and Peng 2011).

Within emerging countries, most public firms are family owned, and the identity of large owners often determines the control structure of the firm. Family owners are more reluctant to draw equity from the stock market, fearing loss of control and family cohesiveness (Thomsen and Pedersen 2000). When families appoint an owner CEO, they have an information advantage over minority shareholders (Anderson and Reeb 2003a). In family-owned and -managed firms, the sharing of sensitive information with outside managers and investors is unlikely because of the weak institutional environment. Hence, the controlling family and its members serving in top management roles have information advantage over minority shareholders. Corporate governance practices designed to protect minority shareholders in Latin America are minimal (Castro, Brown, and Baez-Diaz 2009); more than 40 percent of the firms in this study did not have independent directors, and eight out of nine board members were insiders (they reclassified gray/affiliated directors—*those with a business or family relationship to key shareholders*—as insiders). These numbers probably reflect the degree of control that families still have on Latin American firms. In this same study, 79 percent of Mexican firms had a family as its main shareholder. That same figure was 48 and 43 percent for Brazil and Chile, respectively. Finally, these authors find that in Mexico 48 percent of sampled firms have a dual share structure. For Brazil it is 14 percent and for Chile 7 percent. A dual share structure means that there are two types of stock per firm: one with voting and the other without voting rights. This strategy is often used when controlling shareholders want to maintain control and can exacerbate conflicts between majority and minority shareholders.

Weak institutions contribute to the intervention of politicians in business activities (Hellman, Jones, and Kauffman 2000). Politically connected managers and owners can use their influence to reduce regulatory pressures or to gain preferential access to government contracts. On the other hand, politically connected managers and owners could also use the firm and its resources to serve political objectives to the detriment of minority shareholders. Controlling shareholders with political ties in Indonesia prefer the private benefits of control over external financing opportunities, although the latter would be beneficial to all shareholders (Leuz and Oberholzer-Gee 2006). Political connections in family firms can also result in excessive employment or in favoring employees with political connections rather than those that have the necessary skills.

Expropriation of minority shareholders is not easily observed in good times. But, during economic downturns, controlling shareholders may feel tempted to extract firm resources to protect their own wealth (Young et al. 2008). During the 1997 Asian financial crisis, even firms with a good reputation exploited their minority shareholders (Johnson et al. 2000).

Resolving principal–principal conflicts in emerging economies requires creative solutions. An institution-based view of corporate governance suggests that individual countries will need to work out answers appropriate to their own institutional conditions (Peng and Jiang 2010). Eliminating concentrated ownership structures in emerging markets is probably not realistic because of the scarcity in supporting institutions—*takeover markets, effective boards of directors, and rule of law.*

CHAPTER 2

The Mexican Context

The Economy

Mexico's US$2.3 trillion economy is the 11th largest in the world. It has become increasingly oriented toward manufacturing since NAFTA was signed in 1994. Per capita income is roughly one-third that of the United States. Income distribution is highly unequal. The country is now the United States' second-largest export market and third-largest source of imports. Mexico has free trade agreements with 44 countries, and 90 percent of its trade is regulated by these agreements. The country is the 13th largest exporter in the world. In 2017, 81 percent of Mexican exports went to the US market. GDP size has quadrupled since NAFTA was signed in 1994. Mexico manufactures and exports the same amount of goods as the rest of Latin America together (Heritage Foundation 2018).

Mexico's economy has grown slower than most Latin American countries for more than a decade. Obstacles to economic growth include violence from drug cartels, major tax evasion, and trade disputes with the United States and other partners. Mexico suffered its worth slump since 1932 during the financial crisis of 2009.

The economy's recovery was supported by both external and domestic demand. Mexican manufacturers managed to increase their market share in the United States and Canada. A continued inflow of foreign direct investment into manufacturing, especially in the automotive sector, was very important. The gap between Mexican wages and those of rivals such as China has also narrowed, boosting Mexico's competitiveness (BMI Research 2018).

Growth of real GDP slowed in 2013 after debt defaults by the nation's largest homebuilders (Homex & GEO), a drop in public spending, and a slump in exports. Mexico also suffered two hurricanes causing an estimated US$6 billion in damage. Driven mainly by the service sector, the economy improved modestly in 2014 to 2016. Mexico's tax rate is one of the lowest among Organisation for Economic Co-operation and Development (OECD) countries. There are too many tax exemptions, and the tax revenue base is small. A tax reform was enacted in 2014; it substantially raised nonoil revenue and started to cut expenditures. Disparities between a highly productive modern economy in the North and in the Center and a lower productive traditional economy in the South have widened.

Public and private monopolies still dominate a large part of the economy. Former President Felipe Calderon used to say that Mexicans pay on average 50 percent more than US citizens for their daily goods and services. Fortunately, new antitrust regulations have been enacted in the past three years. The recent telecommunications regulation overhaul has led to a substantial fall in prices (up to 75 percent) and a sharp increase in users. The energy reform has significantly increased private investment. These reforms could add as much as an extra one percentage point to the country's annual growth rate. As a result of the energy reform, private oil companies have been allowed to invest in the industry for the first time since 1938. The government expects a decade of annual auctions. By the end of 2019, Mexico plans to have auctioned more than a third of the country's prospective resources.

Overall, Mexico has embraced economic orthodoxy: sound monetary and fiscal policy, open trade, investment in education, and, more recently, improved competition policy. Between 1995 and 2015, real GDP per person increased by an annual average of 1.2 percent, less than in any Latin American country except Venezuela. If we consider workers coming into the labor force, Mexico does worse: GDP per worker expanded by just 0.4 percent a year (The Economist 2018).

Institutions

In order to provide an overview of Mexican institutions, we use the Worldwide governance indicators (Kauffman, Kray, and Mastruzzi's 2010) based on World Bank data from 2016. Thus, from a total sample of 214 countries we find that Mexico ranks as:

- 94/214 on voice and accountability. This indicator reflects the ability of citizens to participate in selecting their government. It also measures the extent of freedom of association, expression, and media.
- 43/214 on political stability and absence of violence. This measures perception of the probability that the government will be destabilized or overthrown by unconstitutional or violent means, including domestic violence. A high incidence of drug-related violence is a likely cause for the low score in this indicator.
- 128/214 on government effectiveness. This measures public and civil services quality, the extent of governmental independence from political pressure, quality of policy formulation and implementation, and the credibility of the government's commitment to such policies.
- 138/214 on regulatory quality. Regulatory quality measures government's ability to formulate and implement policies and regulations that promote development of the private sector.
- 71/214 on rule of law. This indicator measures confidence in following societal rules, the quality of contract enforcement by police and courts, and the likelihood of crime and violence.
- 49/214 on corruption. This measures the extent to which public power is applied for private benefit. The perception includes the handling of minor and major corruption cases. Corruption is perceived as a major problem; its costs are estimated to be 9 percent of GDP. More than 40 percent of Mexican businesses admit to paying a bribe. Another related problem is the size of the informal sector; although its size has declined recently, more than half of the workforce is still informal.

In terms of business regulations, the World Bank's doing business report for 2018 finds that Mexico:

- Ranks 49/190 countries sampled. Thus, the country ranks in the first quartile of countries in terms of friendliness for conducting business
- Takes 8 days to start a business and 7.8 associated procedures
- Total tax rate as a percentage of profit is 52.1 percent

- Ranks 62/190 in terms of protection of minority investors
- Takes 341 days to enforce a contract with a 33 percent cost of the associated claim

From the institutional indicators we can conclude that Mexico is not the country that the media often portrays as violent and dangerous. It is true that insecurity and corruption are both key challenges but, according to the indicators presented, the country appears to be doing relatively well when compared to large country samples. For those afraid to visit the country, we can say that according to the UN World Tourism Organization, in 2017 Mexico ranked as the sixth country with the most international visitors (39.3 million). Business indicators represent a less optimistic picture: the country ranks in the 2nd quartile for most measures but is clearly in a context where minority shareholder expropriation (principal–principal problems) can take place given the minority investors' protection ranking (62/190).

According to the taxonomy of institutional systems (Fainshmidt et al. 2018) compiled with data from 68 economies, Mexico belongs to the "family-led" configuration where wealthy and dominant families take a central role in ownership, resource allocation, and management. As such, they constitute the central ordering agents of economic life in their countries. Family-led market economies tend to be latecomers to economic development, and their ventures are often protected by the state (Aguilera and Judge 2014). Family-led capitalism is associated with weak institutional environments where investor protection is low, labor market is inefficient, and financial markets are underdeveloped. That is why "when formal legal and regulatory institutions are dysfunctional, founding families must run their firms directly" (Peng and Jiang 2010).

Please refer to Table 2.1 for a detailed description of the country classification of institutional systems.

Demographics

Mexico's population has been growing steadily. It reached 124 million in 2017. In 2000 it was 103 million. Growth has decreased; the fertility rate fell by more than 50 percent in 1980 to 2016 and now stands at

Table 2.1 Country classification

Market Based	Collaborative	State Led	Fragmented with Fragile State	Family Led	Centralized Tribe	Emergent	Collaborative Agglomerations	Hierarchically Coordinated
Australia	Austria	Argentina	Angola	Algeria	Bahrain	Botswana	Czech Republic	Bulgaria
Canada	Belgium	Bangladesh	Cameroon	Azerbaijan	Iran	Chile	Estonia	Georgia
Ireland	Denmark	Belarus	D.R. Congo	Brazil	Kuwait	Hong Kong	Hungary	Jordan
New Zealand	Finland	China	Egypt	Colombia	Qatar	Israel	Latvia	Kazakhstan
Switzerland	France	India	Ethiopia	*Mexico*	Saudi Arabia	Namibia	Lithuania	Korea (South)
The United Kingdom	Germany	Indonesia	Ghana	Morocco	UAE	Singapore	Poland	Lebanon
The United States	Italy	Malaysia	Kenya	Nigeria		South Africa	Slovak Republic	Romania
	Japan	Mongolia	Rwanda	Peru			Slovenia	Taiwan
	The Netherlands	Pakistan	Senegal	Tunisia				Turkey
	Norway	Philippines	Sudan					Ukraine
	Portugal	Russia	Tanzania					
	Spain	Sri Lanka	Uganda					
	Sweden	Thailand						
		Venezuela						
		Vietnam						

Fainshmidt, S., W.Q. Judge, R.V. Aguilera, and A. Smith. 2018. "Varieties of Institutional Systems: A Contextual Taxonomy of Understudied Countries." *Journal of World Business* 53, no. 3, pp. 307–322.

2.2 births. It is expected to be 2.1 births by 2030. The decline began with the introduction of family planning in the 1980s, but a change in family values is another probable reason according to demographers.

Mexico is set to benefit from favorable demographics: a larger labor force will probably bolster manufacturing consumption. While the country will eventually have to face the problems of an aging population, it is entering a demographic sweet spot where the dependency ratio (the proportion of children and retirees compared to the working age population) has fallen to a record low and will probably continue declining over the next decade. This is due to: i) the sharp drop in Mexico's birth rate in recent decades and ii) fewer workers emigrating to the United States. According to the US Census Bureau, Mexicans account for around one-third of the foreign-born population in the United States, although the immigration wave to the United States has reversed in recent years. The economy then should benefit from a larger workforce and the lower pressure on fiscal expenditures due to a smaller dependent population.

Although Mexican society is still young, it is undergoing an aging process. The median age stood at 29.2 years in 2017—6.1 years more than the figure for 2000. The number of those over 65 years jumped from 5.1 million in 2000 to 8.8 million in 2017 and it will reach 15.0 million by 2030 (BMI Research 2018).

Education

Education in Mexico faces several challenges; attendance at higher levels of schooling remains poor, with a large portion of the population not benefiting from a full education. Education quality lags behind most other OECD countries. Thus, even if children are attending school, they may not be gaining the necessary skills for long-term employment. Powerful unions of teachers have been blocking reforms and calling strikes, and this seriously disrupts students' learning. Having said this, the country enjoys a good level of primary school enrollment and a strong tertiary education sector that produces high numbers of graduates with technical skills.

The OECD better life index of 2016 mentions that poor education attainment within the Mexican labor force is limiting productivity.

Mexico has the third-largest proportion of NEETs (individuals who are neither employed nor in education or training) in the 15 to 29 age bracket of OECD countries, which means that a large section of the youth labor force lacks education and vocational skills. This makes a workforce less employable and increases labor costs for businesses employing Mexican workers. On the other hand, tertiary education in Mexico is one of the best in Latin America; the country produces a large number of graduates in engineering and the sciences, which leads to a large pool of workers available for technical positions such as those found in the country's key industries like electronics, auto parts, aerospace, and oil and gas. The main risk for the tertiary sector is the low enrollment rate that is slowly increasing (from 23.3 percent to 29.9 percent in 2014). Out of 588,000 graduates in 2014, 23 percent graduated from engineering, manufacturing, or construction, with an additional 5 percent in mathematics, science, or information systems. Graduates in these fields are highly sought after by foreign investors for technical positions. Mexico currently has two universities listed in the Times Higher Education World University Rankings, the Universidad Nacional Autónoma de México (UNAM) and Tecnológico de Monterrey (ITESM), which are ranked in the 401 to 500 and 501 to 600 ranges, respectively, out of 800 institutions sampled.

Even though the country has challenges in terms of primary and secondary education, it seems to fare well in the tertiary sector from where most firms recruit talent. Hence, these figures could provide a clearer picture for a firm that is considering investing/expanding their business investments in the country. After NAFTA, Mexico has managed to transform itself from a commodity to a manufacturing-based economy, and the quality of undergraduate education seems to have been a part of this virtuous cycle.

Culture

Power distance in Mexico is high. This means that power in society is accepted to be distributed unequally and, because of this, the country exhibits a relatively nonegalitarian executive compensation system where CEOs on average make 45 times the average worker's salary compared to Europe's 26 times (Gomez-Mejia, Berrone, and Franco-Santos 2010).

Variable compensation has grown in importance but it still comprises less than half of total compensation of CEOs and top management teams (TMTs). Equity incentives are used by a small but growing portion of firms.

The country ranks low in individualism, which means that Mexicans prefer to be part of a group. They also prefer to follow traditional gender roles when social duties are distributed. There is also a low tolerance for uncertainty and unpredictability.

In terms of expected leadership qualities, a Mexican leader should be charismatic; one of his/her main challenges is to inspire and motivate others to accomplish group goals. A leader is also expected to involve others when important decisions need to be made. Finally, teamwork for Mexicans does not represent an obstacle; it is a fairly developed philosophy.

CHAPTER 3

The Mexican Governance Model: A Comparative Perspective

Understanding how well investors/shareholders are protected from expropriation by insiders—*managers and controlling shareholders*—is crucial to understand corporate governance in a given country. Legal frameworks influence the intensity of principal–principal problems within stakeholders and the effectiveness of internal corporate governance mechanisms in safeguarding them (Kumar and Zattoni 2016). Legal protection contributes to explain important differences among countries; ownership concentration, dividend policy, and access to finance, for example, are all influenced by legal protection. Because investors finance firms but do not run them, they face the risk of not seeing their returns materialized in the absence of this protection. Corporate governance is, to a large extent, a set of mechanisms that protect investors/shareholders against expropriation by large shareholders and managers (La Porta et al. 2000). Hard and soft (code best practices) mechanisms of law represent a country's combination of formal and informal institutions that guide firms and boards in taking decisions in uncertain environments (North 1990). When corporate governance mechanisms function properly, the contribution of corporations to national income and economic wealth grows, and the corporate governance system is perceived as positive and legitimate (Judge, Douglas, and Kutan 2008). Conversely, when the corporate governance system is dysfunctional, the contribution of firms to wealth creation stagnates. Hence, *in order to understand the influence of institutions on corporate governance*, we believe it is important to provide the reader with data from the World Competitiveness Yearbook survey for the period 2004 to 2014. Our focus will be in analyzing country-level indexes for Mexico and its major trading partners. In Table 3.1 we can see a definition of the studied variables.

Table 3.1 **Variables**

Variable Name	Definition
Corporate Governance Legitimacy Index—OUTCOME-DEPENDENT	Refers to a composite factor score between two variables: corporate boards and investor rights protection. A higher value of this indicator reflects a higher level of protection for investors and board of directors' conflict-solving capacity.
Personal Security and Private Property Rights—REGULATORY	Personal security and private property rights are protected by the law and governmental institutions.
Audit and Accounting Practices—NORMATIVE	Auditing and accounting practices are implemented in business.
Social Responsibility—CULTURAL	Business practices are perceived to be socially responsible.

Note: Factors are quantified in intervals from 0 to 10 where 0 refers to total disagreement with the attribute and 10 total agreement.
Source: World Competitiveness Yearbook Data. 2004-2014. IMD. Geneva; Rivas, J.L., and Rubio J. 2017. "Institutions and Corporate Governance Legitimacy: A Cross Country Study." *Academy of Management Proceedings* 2017, no. 1.

Corporate governance systems can show the convergence of macro-institutions in different countries (De Kluyver 2009). Variables within our sample capture the stage of development for property rights, the strength and applicability of audit and accounting practices, and, finally, the perception of socially responsible practices. Overall, we expect high scores on the above-mentioned factors to be related with corporate governance legitimacy. Country scores for each variable are listed in Table 3.2.

The major weakness for Mexico seems to be in both property rights and audit and accounting. This is probably related to the country's ever-lasting institutional deficit: the establishment of a solid rule of law and law-abiding mechanisms in both criminal and civil justice procedures.

Recent academic studies have reported a high incidence of businesses engaging in illegal acts and corruption. For example, the second edition of the study "Mexico: Anatomy of Corruption" published by Instituto Mexicano para la Competititivdad (IMCO) and Centro de Investig-ación y Docencia Económica (CIDE), released in 2016, revealed that

Table 3.2 Country results (World Competitiveness Yearbook 2004-14; Rivas & Rubio 2017)

Variable	CGLIndex	PROPRIGHTS	AUDIT_ACC	CSR
Mexico	6.19	4.75	6.19	4.75
Brazil	6.8	5.59	6.80	5.59
Canada	7.87	6.72	7.87	6.72
China	5.51	5.40	5.51	5.4
Germany	7.66	5.96	7.66	5.96
Japan	6.56	6.73	6.56	6.73
South Korea	5.89	5.82	5.89	5.82
Spain	6.75	4.61	6.75	4.61
The United Kingdom	7.2	5.46	7.2	5.46
The United States	7.16	5.77	7.16	5.77

CGL: Corporate Governance Legitimacy; CSR: Corporate Social Responsibility

43 percent of established enterprises have paid bribes in order to speed up administrative procedures, gain market share from rivals, or getting concessions and permits to start or maintain its operations (Casar 2016). The report also found that around 82 percent of business executives in Mexico agreed with the notion that illegal acts are carried out extensively when doing business in the country, calling attention to the fact that only 48 percent of economic wrongdoings are ever detected or filled by anticorruption bodies. Mexico is also at the top of the list in terms of sanctions by the Foreign Corrupt Practices Act in Latin America. The unfinished "National System against Corruption" increases transparency and accountability of public servants and will apply sanctions to individuals from both the private and public sectors (PricewaterhouseCoopers 2018). This environment has been detrimental to business development and entrepreneurship by raising the costs of doing business. For example, according to estimates from economic think tank Mèxico, ¿Como Vamos? the country loses 2 percent of GDP per annum or around MXN 340 billion due to corruption (Franco 2015). Overall, Mexico's formal regulatory reform toward higher quality in governance mechanisms and competitiveness has not been met with a corruption decrease, and this could very likely be the reason for its low scores in corporate governance legitimacy.

By illustrating how institutions can influence country-level corporate governance, readers can have a better understanding of how policy makers can contribute to improve corporate governance perceptions within a country.

CHAPTER 4

Corporate Governance in Mexico

Mexico was a land inhabited by various indigenous civilizations (i.e., Mayas, Aztecs). It was conquered by the Spanish captain Hernán Cortes in 1521. The country today is a blend of its history; 80 percent of its population is a racial mix between the Spanish and the native cultures. It is mostly a collectivist culture that is socially cohesive. It is, thus, a traditionalist society where family, religion, and culture play a key role.

The legal system is based in civil law as for most former colonial members of the Spanish empire. The role of the marketplace is constrained by the government and local interest groups such as unions, political parties, commerce chambers, and private firms. Because of this, the market for corporate control is weak and almost nonexistent. Corporate governance codes are voluntary, although they are being slowly incorporated into securities laws.

Corporate ownership in most firms is concentrated and institutional investors—even though present—are still not major players in the market for corporate control. Minority ownership is protected for the standard of an emerging economy. Shareholder activism is uncommon. Corporate boards are single tier in nature, and it is common to have CEO duality where the CEO is also chairman of the board. Corporate boards are made mostly of insiders and representatives of the controlling shareholders. Independent board members have grown in importance, but they still do not hold majority stakes for most firms.

The Mexican Stock Exchange formally opened in 1895. In 1905, it was quoting around 60 mining firms, 30 industrial firms, and 20 banks. Modern stock trading did not begin until 1933 through the creation of the CNBV—*National Banking and Stock Market Commission*—which would serve as its main regulatory body. Until the mid-1970s the stock market did not represent an important source of financing for firms (most financing was provided by banks and state-owned financial institutions) but, in 1975 a new stock market law that fostered the institutionalization of brokerage firms emerged. This law along with the oil market boom that lasted until 1979 multiplied the stock market index by six. Then came a crash and the economy encountered additional problems that ended with the nationalization of banks in 1982. Probably as a result of these shortcomings, market capitalization of the stock market went from 10 percent of GDP in 1978 to 1 percent in 1982. It then fluctuated from 1 to 2 percent of GDP until 1987 (Bebczuk et al. 2007).

In 1985, Mexico joined the General Agreement on Tariffs and Trade (GATT). In 1993 it signed NAFTA with Canada and the United States. Along with the liberalization of trade, the government implemented a far-reaching fiscal reform. Most state-owned firms were privatized, and their number decreased from 1,155 in 1982 to 220 in 1993. Income tax was reduced from 42 to 34 percent and tax compliance was enforced. Government subsidies were notably decreased. These reforms helped in changing the primary fiscal balance from negative (1970 to 1982) to positive (1983 to 1993).

Corporate Law

There are two basic laws that deal with firm corporate governance. One is the Law of Mercantile Societies (1934) dealing with the creation of a limited liability firm—*sociedad anónima*. It establishes investor's property rights and the regulation of different monitoring and counseling bodies of the firm, such as the board of directors, stockholder's assembly, auditor, and a commissioner. This law applies to all private firms in the country. The second one is from 2005 and applies to firms listed in the stock exchange. It is the Law of Securities Markets. When the 2005 edition of this law was approved, it had two objectives that distinguished it from its 2001 version: one, to promote the introduction of new firms to public markets by simplifying regulations and making mid-size firms more attractive to venture capital; and two, to improve transparency, minority rights, and corporate structure of listed firms. Private firms are obliged to follow the 1934 law where the board of directors is mostly responsible for operating a firm. The traditional monitoring role of a board in the 1934 law corresponds to a statutory auditor that reports directly to the shareholder assembly. Many private firms have voluntarily instituted practices from the Law of Securities Markets but they still need to comply with the Law of Mercantile Societies from 1934. The updated 2005 version of the law for securities markets emphasizes a proper identification of controversial matters and excess risks, compliance with norms related to audit matters, and the vigilance of mechanisms that promote transparency. An important issue is the creation of the audit and corporate practice committees that must be wholly formed by outsiders with three members each. The corporate practices committee has a say on transactions with related parties and reviews TMT compensation policies including loans and nonmonetary compensation. It also convenes all shareholders assemblies.

The external auditor figure must inform the Mexican Securities and Exchange Commission (CNBV) of any issue that threatens corporate stability. External auditors must meet a specific set of personal and professional requirements. They are now liable for any harm caused to firms by their misreporting. The CEO—*Director General*—is responsible for implementing all agreements made in the shareholders' assembly and must set guidelines for control and audit procedures. It is now also mandatory for the CEO to rubricate financial statements as well as any relevant economic and legal information.

Top managers and board members now have a duty of loyalty to the firm. Thus, its members must act in good faith instituting shareholder value maximization policies. A breach to the duty of loyalty will occur with a conflict of interest whereby a group of executives or shareholders is benefited at the expense of others. Another possible breach of loyalty could occur if inadequate transactions are approved.

The board of directors in the new law is a one-tier board appointed by the shareholders with a maximum of 21 members. There is a possibility to designate proprietary and substitute board members. Proprietary members are the "owners" of the board seat notwithstanding their share of the firm capital. Proprietary members designate their substitutes subject to board approval. Public boards should have a minimum of 25 percent independent members. They require at least one audit and corporate practice committee wholly made of independent members. There should be a minimum of four meetings per year. Minority shareholders representing 25 percent of capital can designate at least one board member if the board is made of at least three members. If the firm is public, the ownership stake is decreased to 10 percent. In its annual meeting, shareholders must define policies for the use of firm assets, board member nominations, and internal audit systems. Boards oversee strategy and internal control procedures, supervise top management, approve financial statements, set top management compensation packages, and authorize relevant/related transactions. Likewise, this new law helped improve compliance with audit procedures and prevent conflict of interests by mandating that CEOs rubricate financial statements as well as any other relevant economic and legal information.

Half of the board members should be present in each meeting to have legal quorum. Each board member has one vote. The law allows boards to take decisions without meeting, but this must be expressly allowed in each firm's statutes, and there should be unanimous voting among board members on the issues. The chairman of the board has a "golden" vote in case of ties and does not represent the shareholders but the board itself.

A majority of the new governance reforms in the country are related to digitalization of processes, consolidation of procedures, and improvements resulting from the implementation of oral proceedings for commercial disputes. As a result, Mexico climbed four positions to the 57th place in the 2015 Global Competitiveness Index published by the World Economic Forum, mainly because of reforms in the areas of financial market development and business sophistication. The country has ranked above the average of Latin American countries in indicators such as Contract Enforceability, Minority Shareholders Rights Protection, and Access to Firm Credit.

The Code of Good Governance

The adoption of governance codes and committees has been a steady trend in the past two decades. As in other countries, crises partially triggered the code's evolution.

First came the Mexican financial crisis of 1994. A lack of adequate mechanisms to regulate firm indebtedness as well as the supervision of loan portfolios from financial institutions contributed to worsening a vicious circle created by excessive risk exposure to foreign currencies by both firms and banks.

Then came the East Asian crisis of 1997 to 1998. A committee of Best Corporate Practices was created to pool resources from the private and public sectors. It was a multidisciplinary group that included academics, controlling shareholders, managers, and representatives of the finance, legal, and accounting professions. This was the first effort of its kind in Latin America, and one of the first in the world since it happened right before the US governance scandals of Enron and WorldCom. At that time, only the United Kingdom and a handful of countries had implemented similar efforts to foster transparency within financial markets.

As a result of this effort, in 1999 the committee published a code of best practices that included a series of recommendations of what was then considered best corporate governance practices. The philosophical principle underlying these codes is that disclosure of information on governance practices and investor protection allows markets to distinguish differences among firm policies. Ideally, this information should allow shareholders and potential investors to notice which firms adhere to investor protections, and consequently, those firms with better practices should be able to access capital at a lower cost because they are providing more environmental certainty. These fell into four main areas: i) information disclosure regarding administrative structure, objectives, and procedures of board committees, ii) existence of adequate channels for disclosure of financial information, iii) adequacy of communication between management and board members, and iv) protection of shareholder rights. All firms with public traded securities (debt and equity) need to disclose their information. Analysts and market participants can request specific information and constantly monitor the veracity of firm information. The reputation loss from untruthful answers could be significant due to this verification process by market participants. Information needs to be published as part of a firm's annual report, which is usually approved by the board of directors. The code's recommendations can be applied to governmental, nonprofit, small, or medium firms. Most other codes tend to focus only on medium and large publicly listed firms.

The code was revised in 2006 with an emphasis on board roles and a recommendation to issue ethics and social responsibility codes. In 2010, it was revised for a second time. Among its key recommendations are that board size should be from 3 to 15 members, with 25 percent of them being independent; the elimination of substitute board member figure; a reliance on outside support for audit, finance, planning, compensation practices, and policies; and finally, the supervision of: i) firms' strategic vision, ii) CEO, TMT, and directors' performance reviews, iii) protection of shareholder rights, iv) instituting information transparency and accuracy, v) the existence of internal control mechanisms and the approval of relevant/related transactions, vi) succession plans for CEO and TMTs, vii) contingency and information recovery plans, viii) assessment of compensation plans of CEOs prior to his/her entry, ix) instituting a policy for CEO and TMT compensation and termination packages, and finally, x) an adequate framework to analyze and review firm risks. The code was also updated in 2018 in order to include principles of fiduciary duty and risk. It also recommends to include the following policies: i) prevent and solve disagreements between directors and shareholders, ii) recruitment, hiring, evaluation, and compensation of directors, iii) designate family board representatives, iv) increase the proportion of female directors, v) ensure that the organization's talent and structure are aligned to the strategic plan, vi) update ethics code as well as the unlawful act procedure/ hotline, vii) the existence of an agreement within controlling shareholder families that delineates a procedure to designate their board representatives, viii) disclosure in the annual report of policies used for remuneration packages of CEO and top managers, ix) analysis of strategic risks, and x) disclosure of legal liabilities.

Laws regulating financial entities have recently included some of the codes' recommendations. Namely, the size (3 to 15 members) and independent members (25 percent) plus other best practices such as i) shareholders with 10 percent of capital have the right to designate at least one board member; ii) boards should meet at least every three months with the presence of at least one of the independent board members; and finally iii) the existence of board audit and compliance—*legal*—committees.

Chong, Guillen, and Lopez de Silanes (2009) did an analysis of the 150 public firms in 2003 to 2004 and found that the mean company in Mexico met 78.4 percent of the code recommendations. The range of scores went from 30 to 98.2 percent. They additionally show how the number of recommendations met by the average public firm has increased over time; in 2000—*the first year of the code,* the average firm followed 64 percent of the principles, while the following year the number increased to 70 percent. There were smaller increases in 2002 to 2004, leaving the total compliance score at 77 percent. Both equity and debt issuers must comply with the code. Interestingly, compliance is higher among equity issuers; in 2004 they met 81 versus 65 percent of recommendations for debt issuers.

Alternative evidence of the code's influence can be found in the 2013 editions of best governance practices of Mexican firms from Deloitte: 97 percent of the 394 public and private firms in its sample reported having a board of directors, practically unchanged from the 2009 data. Concurrently, 62 percent of those firms also have an Audit Committee (vs. 54 percent in 2010), and 35 percent reported the establishment of a Risk Policy Committee (vs. 27 percent in 2010). Mexican firms coming from industries such as auto manufacturing and energy have shown the highest rates of institutionalization for governance committees in recent years, a trend directly related to increased international competition and risk-management structures in these capital-intensive sectors (PricewaterhouseCoopers 2015).

The Equity Market

Market capitalization and the number of public firms in the Mexican stock market have not changed much over the years as we can see in Figures 4.1 and 4.2. However, the legal requirements and costs of doing an initial public offering (IPO) have changed for good. Firms aspiring

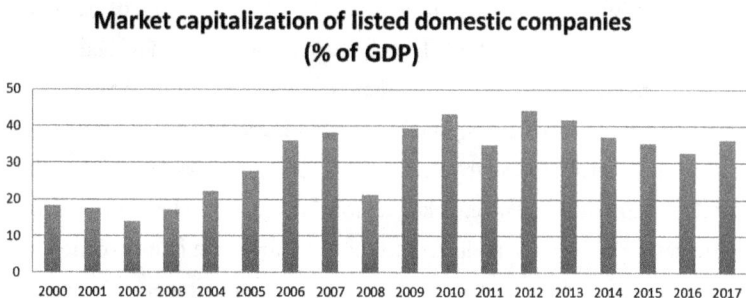

Market capitalization of listed domestic companies (% of GDP)

Figure 4.1 Market capitalization (GDP) in Mexico

Number of Listed Domestic Companies

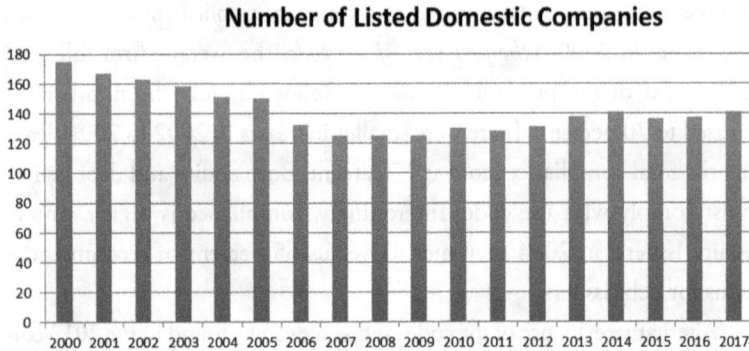

Figure 4.2 *Number of public firms in Mexico (2000 to 2017)*

to be listed must produce a prospectus complying with the rules of the Mexican Securities and Exchange Commission (i.e., Comisión Nacional Bancaria y de Valores: CNBV). The prospectus must largely comment on the intended use of newly raised funds and provide detailed information on the firm, its subsidiaries, and controlling shareholders. CNBV will verify the comprehensiveness of the prospectus and grant permission to trade after approving the document. Listed companies should comply with both listing and ongoing requirements.

The main listing requirements for an IPO company are: three years of operations history, a minimum stockholder's equity value of US$6,321,138 (as of December 2018), positive net earnings for the past three years, a minimum free float of 15 percent of common stock and to issue at least 10,000,000 shares with 200 different shareholders, and a minimum stock price of US$0.3160. The requirement of three years of positive earnings means that small and young Mexican firms face large barriers to equity capital relative to similar firms in the United States or the United Kingdom.

Demand for equity shares in Mexico is limited by a lack of participation of institutional investors. The private pension system has legal restrictions on investments in equity markets (CONSAR 2017). According to the World Bank in its *Doing Business 2015 report*, shareholder right protection in Mexico is similar to that of OECD countries and higher than the Latin American average. A key reason for the limited supply of equity is the nature of its ownership structure; most firms are family owned and Mexico is one of the countries with the highest family ownership concentration globally (La Porta, Lopez de Silanes, and Shleifer 1998).

Among the reasons inhibiting new firm listing are: i) the stock exchange is perceived as a club of "big" firms, ii) revealing firm information can alert competitors, iii) going public might mean losing control, iv) the required changes to internal control and governance mechanisms are expensive and time consuming, v) revealing ownership details might be dangerous due to the prevalent sense of insecurity, vi) tax avoidance schemes that could be revealed, and finally vii) the loss of flexibility to compete against informal competitors.

Business Groups

Business groups are formed by legally independent firms that are bound together by formal and informal ties and are accustomed to taking coordinated action (Khanna and Rivkin 2001). Because government bureaucrats in emerging countries enjoy a great deal of discretion as to how regulations are enforced, groups may have the experience, size, and political connections to navigate in these environments (Khanna and Palepu 1999).

Coordination within business groups relies on a complex web of mechanisms like equity, debt, commercial ties, and relationships between top managers and board members. Business groups owe their predominance to market failures and poor-quality institutions (Granovetter 2005). According to Strachan (1979), business groups have three characteristics: i) diverse set of businesses in different industries; ii) pluralistic composition, meaning that groups are made of more than one family; and iii) a "fiduciary" ambiance where loyalty and trust associated with family values are present.

Groups typically pull resources and top managers from more than one family. They also tend to form either a bank or a financial institution in order to access capital from sources outside their own circle. They are also likely to have oligopolistic market power partially due to their political influence and overinvestment that preventively blocks new entrants and grants them growth spaces for future business.

The advantages of diversified business groups could decrease as stronger institutions are formed in developing countries and countries open their borders to foreign competition. Pointing in this direction, Guillen (2000) found that in situations where governments privilege specific entrepreneurs and restrict access to foreigners, business groups grow.

In a more detailed study, Khanna and Yafeh (2007) found that capital market under development is not a main driver of business group growth. Instead, it is other types of institutions like vague labor laws, low-skilled workers and managers, or the ambition to decrease taxes that are more important. There is also no clear correlation between greater diversification and profits.

Keiretsu in Japan and chaebols in South Korea are synonyms for "grupos" in Latin America. Grupos dominate a significant part of Latin American business, so understanding their characteristics is important for those competing in the region.

Business group development in Mexico is similar to that of other Latin American countries. Groups appeared in the early industrialization period of the late 19th century by creating large manufacturing entities that were stand-alone entities but were financed by banks owned by the same shareholders. They enjoyed a second growth period after 1930 where a network of firms was held together by holding companies. In the third growth period, business groups grew as part of the neoliberal restructuring that started in the 1980s (Del Hierro and Alarco Tosoni 2010). It is important to note that none of the large Mexican groups had a significant place in the high-technology sectors (Salas-Porras 2006b).

For the United States, Mexico and its "grupos" have become important for several reasons: a 2,000-mile border; a growing amount of trade, investments, and bilateral agreements; as well as the fact that there are 36 million Hispanics with a Mexican origin (Pew Research Center 2017).

Tables 4.1 and 4.2 provide data for the ten largest business groups in Mexico for 2008 and 2015, respectively. The list was compiled using the Expansion ranking for Mexico's largest firms. This ranking includes public, private, state-owned, and multinational subsidiaries.

It is interesting to note that:

- The relative importance (measured by sales) of business groups within the largest firms is exactly the same in 2008 and in 2015: 42 percent.
- Walmex—*Wal-Mart's Mexican subsidiary*—is #3 in 2008 and #2 in 2015. Wal-Mart entered Mexico through the acquisition of CIFRA, which was a family-owned public firm in 1997.

Table 4.1 Business groups 2008

BusGroup	#Firms	Group Name	Total Sales USD	Total Firms' Sales USD	%BusGroup	%TotBusGroups
		AMÉRICA MÓVIL	27,969.46		38.6%	
		TELÉFONOS DE MÉXICO	11,738.57		16.2%	
		TELCEL	11,382.19		15.7%	
		GRUPO CARSO	6,730.08		9.3%	
CARSO D	10	TELMEX INTERNACIONAL	6,082.59	72,432.53	8.4%	37%
		CONDUMEX	2,827.30		3.9%	
		GRUPO SANBORNS	2,788.51		3.8%	
		GRUPO FINANCIERO INBURSA	1,509.71		2.1%	
		CICSA	1,154.71		1.6%	
		IDEAL	249.41		0.3%	
		FOMENTO ECONÓMICO MÉXICANO	13,245.61		57%	
Femsa D	3	COCA-COLA FEMSA	6,216.43	23,241.48	27%	12%
		FEMSA COMERCIO (OXXO)	3,779.44		16%	
Walmex F	1	WAL-MART DE MÉXICO	20,195.37	20,195.37	100%	10%
		GRUPO ALFA	9,590.01		49%	
		ALPEK	4,016.70		20%	
Alfa D	5	NEMAK	2,901.53	19,674.50	15%	10%
		SIGMA	2,071.96		11%	
		AXTEL	1,094.31		6%	

(Continued)

Table 4.1 Business groups 2008 (Continued)

BusGroup	#Firms	Group Name	Total Sales USD	Total Firms' Sales USD	%BusGroup	%TotBusGroups
BAL D	6	GRUPO BAL	7,622.53	19,450.83	39%	10%
		INDUSTRIAS PEÑOLES	4,015.31		21%	
		MET-MEX PEÑOLES	3,834.30		20%	
		GRUPO NACIONAL PROVINCIAL	2,230.29		11%	
		GRUPO PALACIO DE HIERRO	1,112.80		6%	
		GRUPO FRESNILLO	635.61		3%	
Salinas D	5	GRUPO SALINAS	5,509.87	13,096.63	42%	7%
		GRUPO ELEKTRA	3,503.39		27%	
		TIENDAS ELEKTRA	1,729.47		13%	
		BANCO AZTECA	1,500.89		11%	
		TV AZTECA	853.01		7%	
GIMM D	3	GRUPO MÉXICO	7,135.57	10,976.64	65%	6%
		MINERA MÉXICO	2,850.50		26%	
		FERROMEX	990.57		9%	
Maseca D	4	GRUPO FINANCIERO BANORTE	4,449.71		50%	
		GRUPO MASECA	3,215.08		36%	
		GRUPO INDUSTRIAL MASECA	808.98	8,904.08	9%	5%
		GRUPO FINANCIERO INTERACCIONES	430.31		5%	
Televisa D	2	GRUPO TELEVISA	3,730.83	3,965.27	94%	2%
		CABLEVISIÓN	234.43		6%	
Kaluz D	1	MEXICHEM	2,071.84	2,071.84	100%	1%
D=Domestic	39		%TOT SAMPLE	$194,009		
F=Foreign				42.29		

Source: Rivas, J.L. 2018. Large Firms in Mexico: An Exploratory Study. Working paper.

Table 4.2 Business groups 2015

BusGroup	#Firms	Group Name	Total Sales USD	Total Firms' Sales USD	%BusGroup	%TotBusGroups
CARSO D	7	AMÉRICA MÓVIL	53,653.50	66,608.68	81%	33%
		GRUPO CARSO	5,211.13		8%	
		GRUPO SANBORNS	2,606.10		4%	
		GRUPO FINANCIERO INBURSA	2,432.99		4%	
		CICSA	984.88		1%	
		IDEAL	935.86		1%	
		MINERA FRISCO	784.21		1%	
Walmex F	2	WALMART DE MÉXICO	27,682.38	34,353.83	81%	17%
		SAM'S CLUB	6,671.45		19%	
Alfa D	5	ALFA	14,498.80	29,022.76	50%	14%
		ALPEK	5,444.16		19%	
		SIGMA ALIMENTOS	4,520.23		16%	
		NEMAK	3,889.31		13%	
		AXTEL	670.27		2%	
Femsa D	2	FOMENTO ECONÓMICO MÉXICANO	16,663.44	23,597.28	71%	12%
		FEMSA COMERCIO (OXXO)	6,933.84		29%	
Maseca D	4	GRUMA	3,158.46	11,780.54	27%	6%
		GRUPO FINANCIERO BANORTE	6,863.44		58%	
		GRUPO INDUSTRIAL MASECA	953.45		8%	
		GRUPO FINANCIERO INTERACCIONES	805.19		7%	

(Continued)

Table 4.2 Business groups 2015 (Continued)

BusGroup	#Firms	Group Name	Total Sales USD	Total Firms' Sales USD	%BusGroup	%TotBusGroups
Salinas D	4	GRUPO ELEKTRA	4,685.74	9,822.23	48%	5%
		BANCO AZTECA	2,845.48		29%	
		TIENDAS ELEKTRA	1,473.75		15%	
		AZTECA	817.26		8%	
GIMM D	2	GRUPO MÉXICO	7,849.61	9,178.18	86%	4%
		FERROMEX	1,328.56		14%	
Televisa D	4	GRUPO TELEVISA	5,067.58	8,116.45	62%	4%
		TELEVISA TELECOMUNICACIONES	1,324.31		16%	
		SKY	1,106.81		14%	
		CABLEVISIÓN	617.76		8%	
BAL D	3	INDUSTRIAS PEÑOLES	3,893.46	6,515.50	60%	3%
		GRUPO PALACIO DE HIERRO	1,435.91		22%	
		FRESNILLO PLC	1,186.13		18%	
Kaluz D	2	MEXICHEM	4,699.92	5,669.61	83%	3%
		ELEMENTIA	969.69		17%	
D=Domestic	35		TOTAL	204,665.07		
F=Foreign			%TOT SAMPLE	42.29		

Source: Rivas, J.L. 2018. "Large Firms in Mexico: An Exploratory Study." Working paper.

- Carlo's Slim group—*Carso*—occupies the first place in both periods, although its relative importance decreased from 37 percent of total business group sales to 33 percent.
- Alfa and Femsa, which represent the Monterrey cluster of firms, account for 22 percent and 26 percent of business group sales, respectively.
- The sample is pretty stable. No newcomers, no departures.
- There is not a single firm in the business group sample that is devoted to a high-technology industry.
- 40 and 30 percent of business groups, respectively (2008 and 2015), have a financial unit in their group.

A Summary of Recent Studies on Mexico (1998 to 2018)

Ownership of Mexican firms is characterized by predominant family participation and by a high concentration of ownership and control. To retain ownership control, owners issue shares without voting rights and develop pyramidal structures. By doing this, owners can gain access to capital without capital dispersion. González and García-Meca (2014) examine the relationship between internal corporate governance mechanisms and earnings management within a sample of public firms in Argentina, Brazil, Chile, and Mexico from 2006 to 2009. They find that ownership concentration can decrease earnings management when the proportion of shares held by major shareholders is below 35 percent. Also, larger boards increase the possibility of earnings management probably due to the decrease of monitoring of TMTs as a result of inefficient coordination and communication. Furthermore, they recommend that firms abstain from hiring "gray" directors (*those that maintain some kind of family or professional relationship—current or past—with the firm or its owners*) and increase director's rotation by placing limits on their terms. They cite as evidence the fact that only 12 percent of firms in their sample have time limits for external directors. Thus, with time, directors can become "labels" where independence is not an attitude but only an appearance. Finally, these authors find that when a country improves the quality of its formal institutions, a decrease in earnings management also takes place.

Machuga and Teitel (2009) use a nonfinancial sample of 34 Mexican public firms from 1998 to 2002 and find that firms that do not have concentrated family ownership or share directors have greater increases in earnings quality. These authors create a new definition of board independence that excludes family relationships, and when introduced in their sample, they find that 24/34 firms do not comply with the required 25 percent of independence at the board level. They also find a significant overlap across boards of firms with concentrated family ownership. These executives might meet the definition of independence, but the interlocking nature of their boards could probably not be known as "impartial."

Castro et al. (2009) compared public firms from Brazil, Chile, and Mexico in 2001 to 2002 and found that CEOs of Mexican firms stayed on the job for twice as long as the average of their counterparts (12.8 vs. 5.4). CEOs in Mexico also own much larger portions of their firms (17.5 vs. 1.5 percent average). Mexico also has a much larger portion of firms with dual share structure (48 percent vs. 14 in Brazil and 7 in Chile). Furthermore, Mexico has the largest number of firms where CEOs are also board chairpersons—*a practice that is forbidden by law in Chile and England.* Finally, the size of Mexican boards is larger; 11.7 versus 9 for Brazil and 8 members for Chile.

Chong, Guillen and Lopez de Silanes (2009) find that better firm-level corporate governance practices are linked to higher valuations, greater performance, and more dividends. They argue that it is only through the development of efficient institutions and investor protection that firms can secure sustainable long-run access to finance. These authors use the compliance scores from the Mexican code of good governance to assess if there is a performance outcome from the code prescriptions. They find that the average company in Mexico met 78 percent of all recommendations in the code with a minimum score of 30 percent and a maximum of 98 percent. They additionally show how dispersed ownership is a myth; in a typical top 10 global firm, 45 percent of the shares are held by the largest three shareholders. Additionally, the countries with weak investor protection have larger share ownership concentration: Latin American countries have larger ownership concentration than the world average. After Greece and Colombia (68 percent), Mexico has the third-largest ownership concentration in their 45-country sample (67 percent). The percentage of firms from Mexico that are listed in the United States is among the highest in the world (15 percent). Thus, in an environment of weak investor protection, firms try to find ways to access external capital markets.

San Martin-Reyna and Duran-Encalada (2012) contend that families in Mexico play a crucial role in defining corporate governance practices. These authors look at board composition in Mexican public firms from 2005 to 2009 and find that only 20 percent of their sampled firms had a majority of outside directors (*although these outsiders could also be sitting in another firm within the same business group*); 35 percent of board members belong to the chairman's family, and in total, 57 percent are either family or firm insiders. They provide evidence that shows a substitution effect: firms without ownership concentration tend to have more independent board members and higher debt levels. This leads to better financial performance for nonfamily firms. For family firms, both higher debt and more independence lead to negative results. Thus, they conclude, ownership concentration is used as a control device.

CHAPTER 5

Family Involvement

In this chapter, we will deal with the level of involvement in family firms. At the end of this section we will provide the reader with measures from a dataset of Mexico's largest firms in 2015 as listed in Expansion 500. This data was complemented with several hand-collected measures and it describes:

A) Type of firm (state-owned, domestic or multinational subsidiary)
B) Level of family involvement (ownership, boards, and management)
C) ROE (average measure) for 2015 to 2017

Family Firms

Family enterprises are the most prevalent form of business organizations. They represent 90 percent of worldwide firms and employ 60 percent of the global workforce (Gedajlovic et al. 2012; Neckebrouck, Schulze, and Zellweger 2018). They are unique because the governance of these firms is largely determined by the governance of the family behind the family firm. The most important voice in governance is not that of an individual but, rather, of a group of people who are interrelated by blood or marriage. Thus, power allocation within the family, its governance institutions, the interaction among family members and stakeholders, and family characteristics such as size and age are all likely to influence firm outcomes (Bennedsen, Pérez-González, and Wolfenzon 2010).

In family firms, the overlap between emotional and cognitive–practical issues is such that family members notably influence major decisions and strategies of these enterprises and vice versa. A family firm is governed and managed with an intention to shape the vision of the business held by dominant family coalitions in a way that is potentially sustainable across generations. The uniqueness of a family firm comes from how its ownership, governance, management, and succession influence the firms' goals, strategies, and structures and the way in which they are implemented. The family component has a special influence within family firms because the quality of family interactions outside the firm shapes firm outcomes (Chua, Chrisman, and Sharma 1999). The components of involvement most often used for family business research are: ownership, management, and governance.

Academics from various disciplines have been drawn to family business studies in order to understand the determinants and consequences of family involvement in business. How such involvement influences the formation and evolution of family enterprises over time has been a guiding principle; differences and similarities of goals, values, resources, strategies, and performance that distinguish family enterprises from their counterparts have been explored since the early 1950s. The first family business center was established in 1962 in Cleveland, Ohio.

Socioemotional wealth (Gomez-Mejia et al. 2007) can be considered a unifying theoretical lens with which to explore family businesses since it addresses core issues that make family businesses unique.

Research on how family firm decisions affect stakeholders was unimportant within family business scholars. The assumption of profit maximization as the main goal of the firm and shareholders as relevant actors was challenged. Some firms pursue objectives beyond profits acting as a mediating hierarchy that effectively balances stakeholder interests. In the specific case of family firms, they are motivated by nonfinancial aspects, and family owners are committed to preserving their socioemotional wealth (Gomez-Mejia et al. 2011). Family heads are usually driven to protect and enhance their socioemotional endowments. The concept of socioemotional wealth refers to emotional endowments that family owners establish with a given firm and influence their decision-making processes.

Research on the performance of family firms shows that large: i) founder-led firms outperform and ii) CEO family-led firms underperform their nonfamily counterparts (Miller et al. 2007; Bennedsen et al. 2007).

Family in Management

It has been argued that family CEOs do not maximize firm value but rather consume managerial perks and attempt to entrench in their role at the expense of shareholders. But, having a founder CEO probably has intangible nonmonetary benefits since founders tend to work harder than most outsider CEOs (Palia, Ravid, and Wang 2008). This argument has been extended to heirs since family CEOs can become benevolently entrenched through higher levels of effort, social recognition as business leaders, and their tacit knowledge on firm operations (González Ferrero et al. 2010). The nonmonetary benefits families enjoy when one of them is CEO do not necessarily lead to a bad outcome for other shareholders (Burkart, Panunzi, and Shleifer 2003).

Succession is probably the most evident assessment of a firm's governance institutions. It is a powerful force that seems to preserve an instinctual drive. Evidence shows that the selectivity of the college attended by a family CEO can have a significant effect on firm performance; the gap is at least 15 percent of firm value (Pérez-González 2006). Further evidence shows that CEOs selected on primogeniture rules exhibit lower levels of managerial practices and productivity than other firms (Mehrotra et al. 2013). Outsider CEOs perform better than family CEOs (Bloom and Van Reenen 2007). Additional evidence also shows that 37 percent of family firms report conflicts resulting from performance of family members in top management roles (Bennedsen et al. 2007).

Warren Buffet was quoted as saying that "family members in management should be the exception and not the rule. It is like choosing an Olympic team based on the primogeniture of the gold medals from previous Olympic events." Indeed, the family in management problem is exacerbated by talented executives avoiding family firms because of limited opportunities of advancement and lack of objective performance measures (Bloom and Van Reenen 2007; Pérez-González 2006). Chang and Shim (2015) find evidence that firms that transition from family to professional CEOs outperform their family CEO counterparts. This performance improvement is more pronounced when a) families maintain high ownership control and outgoing family CEO does not stay in the firm, b) the transition is from nonfounder to professional CEOs, and c) professional CEOs graduated from elite universities.

Family in Ownership

Ownership concentration provides not only incentives for monitoring management but also opportunities for self-serving behaviors, especially if legal protection of investors is weak. Dominant owners in these environments could increase firm value by appointing a majority outsider board with strong qualifications and committees in order to assure investors that the majority owners will refrain from diverting firm resources. Family control on a firm has shown to be inefficient in rapidly evolving industries where future investments are hard to predict (Burkart, Gromb, and Panunzi 1997). This type of control discourages other stakeholder investments and this is probably why family control is rare in research and development industries (Villalonga and Amit 2008).

Outside the United States and especially in countries with low levels of legal protection for investors, ownership structures often include large controlling shareholders (i.e., families). These block holders usually exercise control by appropriating voting rights that do not coincide with their cash flow rights. This can be done using pyramidal structures and cross-shareholdings. Once a family has sufficient ownership for unchallenged control, it can extract resources for personal benefit including excessive compensation or dividends. Families will even retain a poor performing CEO if private benefits are obtained through control (Anderson and Reeb 2003b). A common problem in this type of environments is tunneling, which benefits controlling shareholders by transferring assets at nonmarket prices (Johnson et al. 2000). According to La Porta, López-de-Silanes, and Shleifer (1998), ownership concentration of the largest three shareholders in Mexico stands at 64 percent (vs. 20 percent in the United States and 40 percent in their sampled countries). Voting rights concentration is 74 percent.

Family in Boards

Boards of family firms can be used to monitor management and can also work to resolve conflicts among family members. They can also be a forum where disagreements with top managers and other insiders are solved.

Sraer and Thesmar (2007) show that family firms often have long-term relationships with their employees and offer contracts with implicit long-term job security. By doing this they are able to attract highly qualified staff and increase productivity. These authors also find that in family firms the impact of industry cycles is softened and families strive to honor the implicit parts of labor contracts serving as mediators in family conflicts. Li and Srinivasan (2011) further show that boards dominated by founding family members offer generous compensation packages to CEOs but they are more likely to replace them for poor performance. Because these founding board members have firm-specific knowledge, this allows them to attract more diligent CEOs. Family directors can better assess if the CEO is acting on the shareholders' best interests and they have longer term investment horizons (Gomez-Mejia, Nunez-Nickel, and Gutierrez 2001). Families that exercise control through a board influence performance and reputation positively and, if the board includes the founder, they outperform other firms (Andres 2008; González et al. 2012; Wang 2006). Finally, there is also evidence showing that family boards can be very sensitive to performance even when the CEO is part of the family (Gonzalez et al. 2015).

Let us now turn to the importance of board outsiders. We mentioned that they could serve as mediators in conflicts between family members and top managers, but few outsiders have a real say in governing a family business. Debt holder monitoring is rare due to family firm's tendency for financial conservatism. Thus, the composition of a family firm board is an essential element to determine their governance quality (Bammens, Voordeckers, and Van Gils 2011).

While family control has mixed results on performance (Filatotchev, Lien and Piesse 2005) and family firms are usually reluctant to appoint independent directors, research has shown that family firms with more independent members perform better than their nonfamily counterparts. Independent members seem to mitigate opportunistic behavior by dominant shareholders (Anderson and Reeb 2004). Independent board members also: i) reduce behavioral tendencies of family leaders to favor the family over the firm (Goel et al. 2013) and ii) enhance group effort and motivation (Bettinelli 2011). Thus, we can say that most evidence points to independent directors as a mechanism that enhances board monitoring capability.

In Table 5.1 we can find average ROE for 2015 to 2018 in descending order and the degree of family involvement in ownership, management,

Table 5.1 *Largest firms by ROE: 2015 to 2018*

Rank 2015	Firm	Net Profit	Total Equity	Employees	ROE	FIO1	FIM1	FIB1	Type	Main Families
229	Pronósticos para la Asistencia Pública	645	384	365	168.03	0.00	0.00	0.00	SOE	
180	Fovissste	2,532	2,073	858	122.12	0.00	0.00	0.00	SOE	Public sector
260	Zurich Santander Seguros México	2,292	3,503	930	65.43	1.00	0.00	0.00	MNS	Grupo Zurich (51%); remaining, Zurich Santander Insurance America
89	Kimberly Clark de México	4,224	6,919	8,109	61.04	0.48	0.09	0.17	DOM	González Laporte family
111	Vitro	9,238	17,644	12,690	52.36	0.39	0.00	0.25	DOM	Garza Sada family
363	Atento Mexicana	255	503	18,626	50.60	1.00	0.00	0.00	MNS	Filial de Atentos España Holdco 5 S.L.U.
159	IDEAL	7,187	14,582	2,710	49.29	0.65	0.00	0.33	DOM	Slim family
305	Acciones y Valores Banamex	2,222	4,580	4,837	48.50	1.00	0.00	0.00	MNS	
382	Profuturo GNP Pensiones	335	717	800	46.65	1.00	0.00	0.25	DOM	Bailléres family
123	Seguros BBVA Bancomer	4,283	9,494	1,162	45.11	1.00	0.00	0.00	MNS	Grupo Financiero BBVA Bancomer (99.99%)
421	HSBC Seguros	1,172	2,847	ND	41.17	0.99	0.00	0.00	MNS	Grupo Financiero HSBC S.A. de C.V. (99.9997%)
343	Afore Banamex	1,599	4,624	3,303	34.59	1.00	0.00	0.00	MNS	

379	NatureSweet México	176	516	6,954	34.04	1.00	0.00	0.00	MNS	Filial de NatureSweet, Ltd (EUA)
387	Afore Profuturo GNP	1,077	3,213	ND	33.52	1.00	0.00	0.27	DOM	Baillères family
209	Corporación Moctezuma	2,979	9,389	1,116	31.73	0.52	0.00	0.25	DOM	Buzzi family and Cannizo family
164	Volaris	2,196	7,363	3,553	29.82	0.49	0.00	0.18	DOM	William A. Franke (49.1%); Blue Sky Investments, Luxemburgo (50.1%)
52	MetLife de México	6,720	23,128	1,964	29.06	0.99	0.00	0.00	MNS	Metropolitan Global Management LLC (99%); MetLife International Holdings LLC (1%)
388	Monex Casa de Bolsa	98	359	170	27.32	0.99	0.00	0.33	DOM	Lagos Dondé family, through Monex Grupo Financiero S.A. de C.V.
432	Casa de Bolsa Banorte Ixe	665	2,510	ND	26.50	0.15	0.00	0.00	DOM	Hank González family
38	Sigma Alimentos	3,968	15,781	40,242	25.14	0.42	0.09	0.00	DOM	Garza Sada family
306	Unifin Financiera	928	3,794	426	24.47	0.54	0.11	0.20	DOM	Lebois Mateos family and Luis Gerardo Barroso González
184	SANLUIS Corporación (Rassini)	1,040	4,301	5,896	24.18	0.40	0.22	0.20	DOM	Madero Bracho family

(Continued)

41

Table 5.1 *Largest firms by ROE: 2015 to 2018 (Continued)*

Rank 2015	Firm	Net Profit	Total Equity	Employees	ROE	FIO1	FIM1	FIB1	Type	Main Families
335	Fonacot	1,747	7,224	1,223	24.18	0.00	0.00	0.00	SOE	Public sector
230	Pensiones Banorte	413	1,718	ND	24.04	0.15	0.00	0.00	DOM	Hank González family
477	Toyota Financial Services México	663	2,788	102	23.77	0.99	0.00	0.00	MNS	Toyota Financial Services International Corporation (99.99%)
153	Gentera	3,244	13,830	17,796	23.46	0.32	0.04	0.08	DOM	Promotora Social México (32.15%)/cuatro consejeros (5.66%)
110	Seguros Banamex	1,800	7,680	450	23.44	0.99	0.00	0.00	MNS	CitiGroup INC
460	Consubanco	543	2,356	349	23.06	0.50	0.00	0.29	DOM	Grupo Consupago (99.99%)
351	Volkswagen Leasing	1,196	5,216	231	22.94	0.99	0.00	0.00	MNS	Volkswagen Financial Services AG (99.99%)
247	BanCoppel	1,137	4,985	9,881	22.81	0.99	0.00	0.33	DOM	Coppel family
457	Value Grupo Financiero	720	3,206	195	22.47	0.10	0.09	0.11	DOM	Carlos Bremer Gutiérrez(10%)
358	Grupo Aeroportuario del Centro Norte	1,380	6,252	1,122	22.08	0.22	0.00	0.17	DOM	Quintana family
141	Seguros Banorte	2,297	10,596	ND	21.67	0.15	0.00	0.00	DOM	Hank González family
495	Zurich Vida Compañía de Seguros	350	1,614	ND	21.66	1.00	0.00	0.00	MNS	

211	Grupo Profuturo	1,480	6,975	4,294	21.22	0.74	0.00	0.25	DOM	Baillères family
376	Crédito Real	1,476	7,116	333	20.74	0.25	0.10	0.23	DOM	Berrondo family and Saiz family
236	Allianz México	358	1,765	395	20.26	0.99	0.00	0.00	MNS	Subsidiary. Allianz of America INC y Allianz SE (99%)
11	Grupo Financiero BBVA Bancomer	35,426	178,337	37,872	19.86	0.99	0.00	0.00	MNS	Banco Bilbao Vizcaya
419	Scotia Inverlat Casa de Bolsa	274	1,380	377	19.85	0.99	0.00	0.00	MNS	Grupo Financiero Scotiabank Inverlat S.A. de C.V. (99.98%)
118	Ferromex	4,204	21,739	7,771	19.34	0.34	0.00	0.10	DOM	Larrea Mota Velasco family
3	Walmart de México	30,054	156,364	229,980	19.22	0.71	0.00	0.00	MNS	
441	Vinte, Viviendas Integrales	323	1,696	2,098	19.04	0.30	0.00	0.09	DOM	Sergio Leal Aguirre and Carlos Alberto Cadena Ortiz de Montellano
497	El Cid Resorts	881	4,627	3,275	19.03	0.74	0.20	0.50	DOM	Berdegue Sacristan family
54	Gruma	3,925	20,793	18,965	18.88	0.53	0.29	0.33	DOM	González Moreno family
362	Afore Sura	1,334	7,145	ND	18.68	1.00	0.00	0.00	MNS	Grupo Sura (Colombia)
156	Grupo Industrial Maseca	1,798	9,697	4,617	18.54	0.45	0.17	0.13	DOM	Hank González family
215	Banregio Grupo Financiero	1,947	11,213	3,558	17.36	0.31	0.25	0.23	DOM	Familia Rivero

(*Continued*)

Table 5.1 Largest firms by ROE: 2015 to 2018 (Continued)

Rank 2015	Firm	Net Profit	Total Equity	Employees	ROE	FIO1	FIM1	FIB1	Type	Main Families
140	Quálitas Compañía de Seguros	846	4,939	3,846	17.12	1.00	0.11	0.08	DOM	Joaquín Brockman Lozano/ Quálitas controladora S.A.B. de C.V. (100%)
240	NR Finance México	2,110	12,336	487	17.10	1.00	0.00	0.00	MNS	NMAC (51%)
151	CICSA	1,179	6,909	10,462	17.06	1.00	0.00	0.17	DOM	Slim family
384	Corpovael	452	2,676	2,223	16.89	0.59	0.27	0.44	DOM	Vaca Elguero family (59.24%) and Javier Cervantes
177	Grupo Financiero Interacciones	2,271	13,897	1,037	16.34	0.69	0.00	0.17	DOM	Hank Rhon family
187	Megacable Holdings	3,318	20,501	15,849	16.18	0.90	0.20	0.64	DOM	Robinson Bours family
239	Pensiones BBVA Bancomer	734	4,575	ND	16.04	1.00	0.00	0.00	MNS	Grupo Financiero BBVA Bancomer
255	Pinfra	3,899	24,892	2,458	15.66	0.43	0.10	0.25	DOM	Peñaloza Alanís family
45	Nemak	4,468	28,836	21,456	15.50	0.56	0.00	0.38	DOM	Garza Sada family
465	Seguros Afirme	104	696	350	14.90	0.50	0.09	0.45	DOM	Villarreal family
433	CF Credit Services	642	4,365	34	14.72	0.99	0.00	0.22	DOM	Slim family
2	América Móvil	32,179	222,172	193,936	14.48	0.50	0.20	0.33	DOM	Slim family
365	ACE Seguros	112	772	ND	14.47	1.00	0.00	0.00	MNS	Chubb INA International Holdings, Ltd (99.99%)

41	Grupo Lala	3,753	25,977	33,583	14.45	0.30	0.00	0.22	DOM	Tricio Haro family
287	Asur	2,942	20,638	992	14.26	0.50	0.00	0.22	DOM	Chico Pardo family
63	Industrias Bachoco	3,904	27,960	25,262	13.96	0.73	0.00	0.73	DOM	Robinson Bours family
385	HDI Seguros	173	1,272	1,100	13.63	1.00	0.00	0.00	MNS	Talanx International Aktiengesellshaft (99.76%)
271	CIBanco	242	1,800	2,362	13.47	1.00	0.00	0.08	DOM	Jorge Rodrigo Mario Rangel de Alba Brunel, owner
24	Infonavit	20,589	153,857	4,567	13.38	0.00	0.00	0.00	SOE	Public sector
34	Grupo Financiero Santander de México	14,624	109,423	17,163	13.36	0.75	0.00	0.00	MNS	Banco Santander
366	Grupo Financiero Mifel	523	3,927	1,000	13.31	0.36	0.25	0.20	DOM	Daniel Becker Felman
69	Grupo Financiero Inbursa	14,119	106,925	9,044	13.20	0.57	0.00	0.20	DOM	Slim family
320	Grupo Ruba	638	4,857	963	13.13	0.46	0.00	0.42	DOM	Terrazas family and Márquez Villalobos family
122	Seguros Inbursa	1,301	9,910	2,033	13.13	0.57	0.00	0.18	DOM	Slim family
31	Grupo Carso	8,519	65,520	73,445	13.00	0.84	0.00	0.50	DOM	Slim family
315	Banjército	1,484	11,480	1,667	12.93	0.00	0.00	0.00	SOE	Banco de Desarrollo (SNC)
225	Concesionaria Mexiquense	4,284	33,219	691	12.90	1.00	0.00	0.00	MNS	OPI, subsidiary OHL México (99.99%)
65	Grupo Sanborns	3,799	29,763	48,725	12.76	0.82	0.11	0.36	DOM	Slim family

(Continued)

45

Table 5.1 *Largest firms by ROE: 2015 to 2018 (Continued)*

Rank 2015	Firm	Net Profit	Total Equity	Employees	ROE	FIO1	FIM1	FIB1	Type	Main Families
22	Grupo Financiero Banorte	17,215	134,908	27,822	12.76	0.15	0.00	0.00	DOM	Carlos Hank González, chairman
291	Grupo Aeroportuario del Pacífico	2,789	21,949	999	12.71	0.33	0.00	0.22	DOM	Larrea Mota Velasco family
32	El Puerto de Liverpool	9,056	71,758	53,863	12.62	0.79	0.00	0.12	DOM	Michel family and Guichard family
293	Grupo Financiero Multiva	598	4,876	959	12.26	0.53	0.00	0.00	DOM	Vázquez Raña family
43	Arca Continental	8,045	65,885	47,628	12.21	0.10	0.08	0.19	DOM	Barragán family and Arizpe family
464	Finamex Casa de Bolsa	219	1,798	269	12.20	0.10	0.08	0.14	DOM	Carrillo Díaz family and Mauricio López Velazco Aguirre
90	Grupo Financiero Scotiabank Inverlat	4,716	39,635	11,108	11.90	0.99	0.00	0.00	MNS	The Bank of Nova Scotia
389	GM Financial de México	848	7,222	207	11.74	1.00	0.00	0.00	MNS	GM Financial Mexico Holdings LLC (99.9%)
206	BanBajío	1,767	15,176	4,166	11.65	0.51	0.00	0.17	DOM	Oñate Ascencio family
307	Grupo Financiero Monex	803	6,903	2,076	11.63	0.10	0.09	0.29	DOM	Lagos Dondé family
18	Grupo México	24,698	213,601	30,152	11.56	0.71	0.17	0.09	DOM	Larrea Mota Velasco family
143	OHL México	7,681	66,781	1,492	11.50	0.47	0.00	0.00	MNS	Grupo OHL

	Company								Ownership
135	Seguros Monterrey New York Life	1,027	8,938	1,498	11.49	1.00	0.00	0.00	MNS	New York Life Enterprises (99.998%)
377	Grupo Bursátil Mexicano GBM	948	8,271	586	11.47	0.04	0.00	0.20	DOM	Rojas Mota Velasco family and De Garay family
272	Corp. Interamericana de Entretenimiento	416	3,650	6,396	11.39	0.15	0.11	0.09	DOM	Luis Alejandro Soberón Kuri
252	Interceramic	332	2,527	4,664	11.34	0.34	0.13	0.45	DOM	Almeida García family
80	Fragua Corporativo	1,016	9,004	29,535	11.28	0.80	0.47	0.71	DOM	Arroyo Chávez family
193	IEnova México	6,056	53,675	691	11.28	0.66	0.00	0.00	MNS	BANAMEX (27.8%); Semco Holding (66.4%)
57	Banco Azteca	1,463	13,115	33,515	11.16	1.00	0.00	0.33	DOM	Salinas Pliego family
179	Grupo Bafar	517	4,791	11,222	10.79	0.51	0.44	0.31	DOM	Baeza Fares family
120	Grupo Gigante	1,897	17,916	24,294	10.59	0.49	0.38	0.31	DOM	Losada Moreno family
162	Grupo Herdez	1,463	13,304	8,231	10.52	0.51	0.27	0.27	DOM	Hernandez-Pons Torres family
67	GNP	838	7,977	6,509	10.51	0.70	0.00	0.25	DOM	Bailléres family
106	Daimler México	824	7,892	6,812	10.44	0.99	0.00	0.00	MNS	Subsidiary. Daimler Canada Investments
286	Afore XXI Banorte	2,478	23,386	ND	10.37	0.15	0.00	0.00	DOM	Hank González family
476	Seguros Argos	38	371	148	10.15	0.49	0.00	0.14	DOM	Jose Luis Llamosas
470	Actinver Casa de Bolsa	139	1,385	1,423	10.01	1.00	0.00	0.09	DOM	Madero Rivero family, Dotson Castrejón family and Cosío Pando family

(*Continued*)

Table 5.1 *Largest firms by ROE: 2015 to 2018 (Continued)*

Rank 2015	Firm	Net Profit	Total Equity	Employees	ROE	FIO1	FIM1	FIB1	Type	Main Families
342	Caterpillar Crédito	777	7,827	ND	9.92	1.00	0.00	0.00	MNS	Caterpillar Financial Services Corporation (99.99%)
424	Grupo Axo	179	1,821	3,203	9.85	0.22	0.14	0.17	DOM	Gómez Martínez family y Alberto Fasja
326	Grupo Accel	265	2,710	3,322	9.79	0.51	0.33	0.36	DOM	Vallina family
5	Fomento Económico Mexicano	24,360	252,716	243,014	9.64	0.39	0.18	0.32	DOM	Garza, Laguera y Gonda families
318	Invex Grupo Financiero	453	4,721	1,070	9.60	0.51	0.11	0.16	DOM	Guichard Michel family
29	Alpek	3,324	35,355	4,823	9.40	0.56	0.13	0.44	DOM	Garza Sada family
108	Alsea	928	9,903	60,187	9.37	0.50	0.06	0.25	DOM	Torrado Martínez family
313	Sanofi México	913	9,850	1,896	9.27	1.00	0.00	0.00	MNS	
40	Ternium México	4,324	46,767	10,177	9.25	0.62	0.00	0.00	MNS	Ternium S.A.
213	Grupo Lamosa	605	6,547	5,755	9.24	0.53	0.20	0.25	DOM	Toussaint Elosúa family
423	General de Seguros	205	2,219	667	9.24	0.85	0.00	0.57	DOM	Escobedo Conover family
15	Grupo Financiero Banamex	16,314	176,936	41,676	9.22	0.99	0.00	0.00	MNS	Citi Holdings
13	Coca-Cola FEMSA	10,607	116,029	81,689	9.14	0.48	0.00	0.26	DOM	Garza, Laguera y Gonda families
456	Valores Mexicanos Casa de Bolsa	110	1,225	166	9.01	1.00	0.00	0.25	DOM	Bailleres family

292	Grupo Minsa	265	2,944	1,647	9.00	0.83	0.00	0.50	DOM	Gómez family
61	Grupo Aeroméxico	1,017	11,440	13,462	8.89	0.41	0.00	0.21	DOM	del Campo family
70	Mabe	730	8,234	17,972	8.82	0.51	0.20	0.25	DOM	Berrondo Avalos family
10	Grupo Bimbo	5,571	63,512	128,883	8.77	0.67	0.11	0.28	DOM	Servitje family
33	Grupo Televisa	8,106	94,574	41,956	8.57	0.15	0.20	0.05	DOM	Azcárraga Jean family
334	Inmuebles Carso	3,354	39,734	1,040	8.55	0.99	0.00	0.30	DOM	Slim family
172	Mapfre	269	3,149	1,476	8.53	1.00	0.00	0.00	MNS	Mapfre Foundation(63.04%) Savings and Loan/Monte de Piedad Madrid (14.98%)
129	Fresnillo PLC	3,536	43,784	3,907	8.08	0.52	0.00	0.17	DOM	Bailléres family
416	Grupo Gicsa	1,902	23,922	835	7.95	0.42	0.20	0.18	DOM	Cababie Daniel family
231	Grupo La Moderna	546	7,050	5,244	7.74	0.51	0.30	0.60	DOM	Monroy family
25	Organización Soriana	3,879	50,219	90,251	7.72	0.57	0.08	0.38	DOM	Martin Bringas family
442	Médica Sur	249	3,223	2,733	7.72	0.50	0.00	0.00	DOM	Neuco S.A. de C.V.
39	Grupo Comercial Chedraui	1,854	24,165	42,825	7.67	0.69	0.21	0.25	DOM	Chedraui family
217	Afirme Grupo Financiero	448	5,539	3,627	7.54	0.98	0.00	0.57	DOM	Villarreal family
337	Peña Verde	305	4,070	36	7.50	0.55	1.00	0.29	DOM	Escobedo family and Lutt-mann Fox family
356	Promotora Ambiental	163	2,402	5,215	7.42	0.57	0.00	0.43	DOM	Garza Santos family

(*Continued*)

Table 5.1 *Largest firms by ROE: 2015 to 2018 (Continued)*

Rank 2015	Firm	Net Profit	Total Equity	Employees	ROE	FIO1	FIM1	FIB1	Type	Main Families
202	Grupo Industrial Saltillo	749	10,181	7,049	7.36	0.42	0.11	0.50	DOM	López family
484	Reaseguradora Patria	130	1,776	78	7.34	0.26	0.09	0.40	DOM	Escobedo Conover family
349	Grupo Financiero Actinver	318	4,568	1,639	6.95	0.10	0.00	0.12	DOM	Madero Rivero family and Valenzuela Rionda family
201	Cablevisión	865	12,785	5,802	6.76	0.51	0.00	0.14	DOM	Azcárraga Jean family
295	Financiera Independencia	254	3,770	11,013	6.73	0.33	0.00	0.43	DOM	Rion Santisteban Cantú family and Guillermo Daniel Barroso
447	Exportadora de Sal	220	3,329	1,337	6.62	0.00	0.00	0.00		
263	Rotoplas	423	6,480	2,406	6.52	0.66	0.13	0.13	DOM	Rojas family
408	Grupo Real Turismo	241	3,748	4,736	6.43	0.29	0.00	0.23	DOM	Vázquez Raña family
224	Seguros Atlas	238	3,706	999	6.41	0.51	0.17	0.44	DOM	Rolando Vega Sáenz
98	Banobras	2,407	37,669	1,000	6.39	0.00	0.00	0.00	SOE	Public sector
199	Grupo Cementos de Chihuahua	920	15,439	2,800	5.96	0.74	0.00	0.20	DOM	Terrazas Becerra family
328	Agroasemex	105	1,792	190	5.84	0.00	0.00	0.00	SOE	Public sector
297	Cydsa	528	9,202	1,570	5.73	0.50	0.13	0.53	DOM	González family

55	Controladora Co-mercial Mexicana	1,578	27,799	22,140	5.68	0.96	0.08	0.38	DOM	Martin Bringas family
134	Nafin	1,441	25,850	1,024	5.57	0.00	0.00	0.00	SOE	Public sector
404	Grupo Financiero Ve por Más	220	3,978	875	5.54	0.39	0.00	0.15	DOM	Del Valle Perochena family
275	Consorcio ARA	607	11,278	8,274	5.38	0.48	0.25	0.18	DOM	Ahumada Russek family
330	Coconal	249	4,730	3,670	5.27	0.25	0.14		DOM	Ovalle family and Lona family
393	Financiera Rural	1,724	33,244	1,312	5.19	0.00	0.00	0.00	SOE	Public sector
359	Bansefi	95	1,930	ND	4.91	0.00	0.00	0.00	SOE	Public sector
86	AXA Seguros	477	9,885	4,014	4.83	1.00	0.00	0.00	MNS	AXA International
154	Elementia	821	17,229	6,218	4.76	0.40	0.00	0.36	DOM	Grupo Kaluz and Del Valle family (39.59%); Holding (35.62%); Remaining, public investors
36	Grupo Elektra	2,593	55,250	69,180	4.69	0.72	0.08	0.38	DOM	Salinas Pliego family
196	Bancomext	941	20,412	556	4.61	0.00	0.00	0.00	SOE	Public sector
44	Industrias Peñoles	3,083	67,339	11,547	4.58	0.69	0.00	0.29	DOM	Baillères family
109	Grupo Palacio de Hierro	725	16,846	12,190	4.30	0.98	0.00	0.33	DOM	Baillères family
35	Mexichem	2,583	63,508	18,986	4.07	0.42	0.00	0.38	DOM	Del Valle Perochena family
426	Grupo Vasconia	69	1,757	1,614	3.95	0.40	0.09	0.15	DOM	Elizondo Anaya family and Maria Isabel Moral Pederzini

(Continued)

Table 5.1 *Largest firms by ROE: 2015 to 2018 (Continued)*

Rank 2015	Firm	Net Profit	Total Equity	Employees	ROE	FIO1	FIM1	FIB1	Type	Main Families
28	Kaluz	3,213	84,714	25,968	3.79	1.00	3.00	3.00	DOM	Del Valle Perochena brothers (control 100%)
6	Alfa	3,152	83,196	74,563	3.79	0.42	0.20	0.09	DOM	Garza Sada, Calderon, Barragan, Garza families
132	Grupo Kuo	313	8,338	18,243	3.76	0.25	0.09	0.25	DOM	Senderos Mestre family (24.5%) and Diaz Elondo family (3%)
73	Grupo Xignux	300	8,085	19,068	3.71	0.36	0.25	0.62	DOM	Eugenio Garza Herrera
439	Corporación Mexicana de Restaurantes	39	1,075	5,628	3.63	0.69	0.09	0.25	DOM	Vargas family
59	Grupo Financiero HSBC	1,930	55,309	16,896	3.49	0.99	0.00	0.00	MNS	
158	Grupo Famsa	340	9,968	17,880	3.41	0.64	0.17	0.50	DOM	Garza Valdez family
436	Grupo Mexicano de Desarrollo	116	3,565	1,725	3.24	0.50	0.14	0.26	DOM	Ballesteros family
284	Red de Carreteras de Occidente	512	18,298	1,086	2.80	0.73	0.00	0.00	MNS	Matador Infra BV (73.24%)
83	Industrias CH	853	37,134	5,490	2.30	0.67	0.67	0.25	DOM	Vigil González family
8	Cemex	3,887	169,555	42,741	2.29	0.15	0.08	0.23	DOM	Zambrano family
327	Compañía Minera Autlán	80	4,469	2,062	1.79	0.90	0.00	0.30	DOM	José Antonio Rivero Larrea and family

96	Grupo Simec	533	30,175	4,342	1.77	0.56	0.00	0.14	DOM	Rufino Vigil González
333	Banco Ahorro Famsa	51	2,889	4,595	1.75	1.00	0.00	0.36	DOM	Garza Valdez family, through Grupo FAMSA S.A.B. de C.V.
329	Eli Lilly de México	54	3,200	885	1.69	1.00	0.00	0.00	MNS	Eli Lily and Company
142	Bio PAPPEL	140	11,217	9,938	1.25	0.74	0.67	0.70	DOM	Rincón Arredondo family/ Grupo Bio Pappel S.A. de C.V. (74.101%), Employees Trust fund (11.131%)
282	Grupo Pochteca	10	1,185	1,419	0.87	0.07	0.09	0.09	DOM	Jorge Gutiérrez Muñoz
443	Crédito Familiar	4	877	ND	0.46	1.00	0.00	0.00	MNS	Scotiabank
189	Farmacias Benavides	1	1,507	9,306	0.04	0.95	0.11	0.14	DOM	José Luis Rojas Toledo
350	Grupo Senda	−15	1,189	7,340	−1.29	0.84	0.00	0.00	DOM	Banco Regional de Monterrey (84%); remaining, Rodríguez Benítez brothers
71	Organización Cultiba	−267	16,697	40,337	−1.60	0.64	0.17	0.24	DOM	Gallardo family
300	Grupo Collado	−16	946	1,657	−1.66	0.51	0.09	0.14	DOM	Vogel family
281	Codere México	−224	7,947	7,600	−2.82	0.17	0.13	0.22	MNS	Codere S.A./José Antonio Martínez Sampedro (14.17%); Javier Martínez Sampedro (2.5%)

(Continued)

Table 5.1 *Largest firms by ROE: 2015 to 2018 (Continued)*

Rank 2015	Firm	Net Profit	Total Equity	Employees	ROE	FIO1	FIM1	FIB1	Type	Main Families
434	Sociedad Financiera Inbursa	−183	5,266	ND	−3.48	1.00	0.00	0.22	DOM	Slim family
66	Aeropuertos y Servicios Auxiliares	−306	8,647	2,402	−3.54	0.00	0.00	0.00	SOE	Public sector
288	Grupo Posadas	−153	4,214	15,194	−3.62	0.12	0.29	0.30	DOM	Azcárraga Andrade family
173	Sociedad Hipotecaria Federal	−755	18,639	448	−4.05	0.00	0.00	0.00	SOE	Public sector
186	Genomma Lab Internacional	−383	8,848	931	−4.33	0.28	0.00	0.18	DOM	Herrera Aspa family
267	Liconsa	−111	1,674	4,692	−6.61	0.00	0.00	0.00	SOE	Public sector
4	Comisión Federal de Electricidad	−21,496	275,396	68,922	−7.81	0.00	0.00	0.00	SOE	Public sector
58	Altos Hornos de México	−2,710	20,475	21,984	−13.24	0.79	0.18	0.43	DOM	Ancira Elizondo family
145	Diconsa	−450	3,326	4,233	−13.52	0.00	0.00	0.00	SOE	Public sector
418	Correos de México	−205	1,296	17,521	−15.82	0.00	0.00	0.00	SOE	Public sector
183	Minera Frisco	−3,416	16,646	6,105	−20.52	0.78	0.00	0.23	DOM	Slim family
352	AIG Seguros México	−182	878	517	−20.77	0.99	0.00	0.00	MNS	AIG Latin America Investments LLC (99%)
174	TV Azteca	−1,850	8,777	4,067	−21.08	0.65	0.20	0.18	DOM	Salinas Pliego family

279	Casas Javer	-282	1,159	1,601	-24.34	0.25	0.00	0.08	DOM	Salomón Marcuschamer Stavchansky
1	Petróleos Mexicanos	-389,751	-1,110,802	139,176	-35.09	0.00	0.00	0.00	SOE	Public sector
413	Maxcom Telecomunicaciones	-999	2,141	1,581	-46.68	0.14	0.00	0.07	DOM	Rodrigo Lebois Mateos and Enrique Castillo Mejorada
194	Axtel	-2,412	4,075	7,128	-59.19	0.10	0.00	0.22	DOM	Garza Sada family
74	Empresas ICA	-7,759	11,880	22,680	-65.31	0.12	0.13	0.11	DOM	Bernardo Quintana
406	Grupo TMM	-665	764	1,607	-87.08	0.36	0.00	0.29	DOM	Serrano family
310	Lotería Nacional para la Asistencia Pública	-136	115	930	-118.31	0.00	0.00	0.00	SOE	Public sector

FIO1	Family in Ownership 1	51.63%
FIM1	Family in Management 1	9.55%
FIB1	Family in Board 1	25.91%
TYPE	Domestic (DOM)	69.9%
	Multinational Subsidiary (MNS)	20.2%
	State Owned (SOE)	6.9%

Source: Annual reports, firm web pages, Expansion, SEC, CNSF, Capital IQ, El Economista, CONDUSEF, www.gob.mx.

and boards for the largest Mexican firms (Expansión magazine 2015). It is worth noting that:

A) 70 percent are domestic firms, 20 percent are multinational subsidiaries, and only 7 percent are state-owned entities
B) Top 2 performing firms are state owned (Pronósticos and Fovissste)
C) 50 percent of the top performers are financial firms
D) 40 percent of bottom performers are state owned
E) The highest performing group in terms of ROE are multinational subsidiaries (18 percent) followed by state-owned entities (13 percent) and domestic firms (9 percent)
F) For domestic firms we find that:
   • Ownership concentration for the first shareholder (family) is 52 percent
   • Average percentage of first family in TMT is 10 percent
   • Average percentage of first family in board is 26 percent

CHAPTER 6

Board Composition in Mexico

Corporate boards usually perform two roles: an advisory role to top management and a monitoring role on behalf of shareholders. The importance of board diversity has been shown both on the monitoring (agency theory) and in the advisory (resource dependence) side. Because diversity brings different viewpoints to the table, a diverse board can more effectively monitor executive behavior.

Board composition is influenced by both firm and country contexts. Industry type, firm size, age, and degree of internationalization as well as country industry structure, history, culture, and institutional strength are all critical to define board structure. In Germany we find union representatives as board members, in Japan it is loyal executive insiders, and in China it is government officials who occupy several board positions. In the United States, boards were traditionally made by the controlling shareholders although this model evolved to the current one where boards now include a majority of independent nonexecutive directors that have the power of making relevant decisions. Globalization has also added pressure to increase foreigners and representatives of institutional investors. Because boards are the highest-level mechanism in a firm to reduce uncertainty and add transparency, firms in need of capital or investors will probably do better if their board is perceived as up to date with board best practices. If we are dealing with firms in an emerging country environment that is usually characterized by institutional weakness and high ownership concentration, true outsider independence, family and government links will play an additional role in what is considered as best practices.

Boards have often been labeled as "supra TMTs" but we argue that they are not really a team; they have distinct features: first, boards often

include "outsiders" who have their primary affiliation with another organization, serve on boards on a part-time basis, and have limited exposure to the firm's affairs. Second, boards average 13 members versus 5.9
for TMTs. Finally, unlike many teams, boards function episodically; full
board meetings are held, on average, 7 times per year. Even considering
committee meetings, board members spend less than 2 weeks per year
working on the boards they serve (Jehn 1995; Monks and Minow 1995).
Boards are then large, elite, and episodic decision-making groups facing
strategic issue-processing tasks. Since they are not involved in implementing their recommendations, their output is entirely cognitive. Also,
because they are large, episodic, and interdependent, they can suffer "process losses," which are interaction difficulties that prevent groups from
achieving their full potential (Forbes and Milliken 1999; Rivas 2012a).

Research has now shown that board characteristics affect acquisitions,
divestitures, diversification, research and development, strategic change,
executive compensation, and CEO dismissal (Deutsch 2005; Golden and
Zajac 2001; Haunschild 1993; Shen and Cannella 2002; Shimizu 2007).

We will now turn to key characteristics of public boards in Mexico
taken from a unique hand-collected dataset of public firms that spans
from 2008 to 2016. For readability purposes, we will only deal with three
years: 2008, 2011, and 2016. Following corporate governance research
practices, we exclude: financial, delisted, and minimum trading firms,
which yields a total of 79 firms. A representation of this data can be found
in Table 6.2.

Foreigners

International membership is an important variable of a board's international background and orientation. Nationality is a source of knowledge on a particular region or economy. Foreign-born board members
possess valuable knowledge on market insights and institutions as well as
on culture, behavior, and norms of a given country. Hence, the nationali-
ties of board members have implications for individual personalities and
team dynamics as well as for strategic decision making. Such knowledge
may prove invaluable in making decisions about firm strategy in a particular region and on international operations, as they connect the firm

with contextual factors in order to decrease uncertainty and dependency. Foreign-born directors should also help in promoting more effective global relationships since cultural sensitivity is critical in an international environment (Carter, Simkins, and Simpson 2003).

In short, we believe that having foreign board directors should decrease uncertainty by enhancing social capital among foreign investors as well as providing knowledge on specific regions or countries.

In Mexico the percentage of board members who are foreigners has slowly gone up; it was 8 percent in 2008, 10 percent in 2011, and 12 percent in 2016.

Women

There is increasing pressure to have female presence on boards in order to reduce the gender gap and increase the diversity degree of boards.

Female directors have unique skills, experience, and networks. They are less prone to risk-taking behavior; firms with female CEOs have lower debt levels, less volatile earnings, and higher survival probabilities than firms led by male CEOs (Faccio, Marchica, and Mura 2014). Women can enhance board independence of thought and monitoring functions. Prior evidence shows that higher female board representation is associated with better attendance by male directors, more board meetings, increase in pay for performance, and more attention to stakeholders (Adams and Ferreira 2009; Adams, Licht, and Sagiv 2011; Rhode and Packel 2014).

Gender diversity has been found to facilitate creativity within groups and also to lead to clashes because others find it difficult to identify with those of a different gender (Nemeth 1992; Pelled, Eisenhardt, and Xin 1999). Thus, gender diversity has positive and negative implications for processes relevant to the board advice and counsel functions (Hillman, Shropshire, and Cannella 2007). However, because boards engage in nonroutine problem solving and meet infrequently, the improved brainstorming and creativity from considering diverse perspectives may represent "functional conflict" (Amason 1996) and benefits that outweigh the negative implications.

From a practical perspective, talented male directors are scarce and institutional investors are increasingly pressing for female directors. Having women on boards might also decrease CEO influence on board oversight, since people of the same race and gender might be less critical of each other's ideas (Erhardt, Werbel, and Shrader 2003).

Gender quotas on boards are generally justified on the basis of business/economic rationale of board diversity. Within the European Union there are now six countries mandating female board representation: Norway (2006—40 percent), Spain (2015—40 percent), France (2017—40 percent), Italy (2012—33 percent), the Netherlands (2016—30 percent), and Belgium (2016—33 percent).

Female board representation is low in Mexico; it was 5 percent in 2008 and 2011 and climbed to 7.6 percent in 2016. This is certainly an area of opportunity for Mexican boards. According to OECD data for large public firms, there are only a few countries in the world that have less female representation than Mexico in 2016:

A) Chile—4.7 percent

B) Japan—3.4 percent

C) South Korea—2.1 percent

D) Brazil—6 percent

E) Indonesia—5.7 percent

Age

Since one of the board's duties is to formulate strategy, director propensity to risk-taking will play an important role upon this duty. An active promotion of age diversity should encourage diverse perspectives and also facilitates board succession planning. Most boards need to have some spread in age: while an older group can provide experience and resources, the middle group can carry more responsibilities, and the younger one provides the energy to move forward. Pointing in this direction, Hacksoon and Chanwoo (2010) found that age diversity at the board level positively affects firm valuation.

Older directors face less career uncertainty and have more experience in making complex decisions. Younger directors, on the other hand, have more energy and drive that could translate into enthusiasm, decisiveness, and ambition. They also have more ideas and are more willing to learn about new technologies in order to make more innovative decisions.

We should also be aware of the downsides of age diversity: communication can become difficult, conflict more likely, and social integration harder to achieve.

Even taking into consideration the above-mentioned downsides, we believe that risk-taking propensity should be counterbalanced with experience, wisdom, and the resources that older members usually have. We argue that with age diversity, boards will be more willing to learn, take risks, and give advice and resources to their respective work groups.

Average age of board members in Mexico is 53, 55, and 57 for 2008, 2011, and 2016, respectively. Although this is consistent with most large developed countries, we need to remember that median age for Mexico's population is 27 (INEGI 2015). Average age also seems high when you consider that research has shown how younger board members provide a board with more risk-taking and energy. If you take a closer look at the age range in Table 6.1, you will see that there is at least one board member both in 2011 and 2016 who is 90 years old, which is far above the standard that many boards use as a maximum to retire their board members. Seventy-three percent of US public boards have mandatory retirement age and their upper limit is 75 years (Spencer Stuart 2017).

Tenure

The length of time that members of a group stay together influences group outcomes, and this might be why tenure is the most studied of all demographic attributes. Long tenures are associated with strategic persistence to a course of action and to stability, reduced conflict, and superior communication (Finkelstein and Hambrick 1990; Katz 1982).

Group longevity can diminish a negative association with emotional conflict by having social categories based on demographic attributes blurred with time. As they develop social and economic ties, group members will likely acquire strong psychological and political commitments to the status quo (Hambrick and Canella 1993). Board members who have served on the same board for a period of time are likely to develop strong friendships and professional ties (Fredrickson, Hambrick, and Baumrin 1988). Therefore, as board tenure increases, directors develop shared beliefs and close friendships. Thus, we believe that having board members with a diverse set of tenures would work well. Older tenured members could provide guidance knowledge and resources, while newer members provide energy and different perspectives to avoid the "groupthink" bias that could stem from groups with similar tenures.

Tenure in Mexico stands at 10, 11, and 11 years for 2008, 2011, and 2016, respectively, which is quite high when you think that there are countries that limit the tenure of independent board members at 8 years. The rationale used for this regulation is that after a certain number of years because of our human nature and the events that surround most board members (meetings, social events, strategic planning retreats) most individuals will stop having an independent attitude.

Duality

CEO duality takes place when the chairman of the board and the CEO are the same person. This is explicitly forbidden by law in some countries (i.e., Chile, the United Kingdom). Generally speaking, it reduces the power balance and accountability between a board and its TMT. But when used for a special purpose, it can provide a firm with advantage. For example, in a developed country context, CEO duality may indeed threaten a firm's legitimacy due to an inherent conflict of interest; the same individual that presides the board and is the ultimate authority in a firm is in charge of monitoring and advising the TMT that includes the CEO. But in emerging country contexts with high macroeconomic volatility where speed and decisiveness in decision making can be crucial, CEO duality can provide a board with greater capability to take decisions.

Duality in Mexico for 2008, 2011 and 2016 stands at 38, 37, and 44 percent respectively, which is high when you think that duality can be forbidden for public firms due to the potential conflict of interest for shareholders and management at the same time. If monitoring, evaluating, and compensating top management is an important board task, how can this be accomplished when the head of the board is also the head of top management?

Independence

The most "recommended" practice of good corporate governance is, still today, that firms institute a board dominated by independent directors.

This comes with a presumption that they can make a positive contribution to the board's monitoring responsibilities and subsequently toward better corporate performance. Having an independent board has been shown to be correlated with less cases of fraudulent financial reporting (Anderson, Mansi, and Reeb 2004; Dunn 2004).

Because of their lack of hierarchical affiliation to management, outsiders may promote the airing of different perspectives and reduce the probability of complacency and narrow-mindedness in board's decision-making processes. Independent directors provide resources to deal with external factors such as the community, buyers, or suppliers, while inside directors serve on boards primarily to provide firm-specific information (Fama and Jensen 1983). Outside directors introduce a balance of power by representing shareholder interests that might not receive the same attention if the board was made mostly of insider or affiliated directors. Because of their lack of hierarchical ties with the TMT, independent directors can become a more impartial body for monitoring behavior.

Independent directors are incentivized to scrutinize management more diligently than other directors since they need to protect their reputation as effective monitors. It is interesting to note that a higher level of board independence has been shown to be influential for firm performance only in the case of emerging countries (Dahya, Dimitrov, and McConnell 2008). Black and Kim (2012) provide evidence in a sample of Korean firms of a stock price increase in boards with a majority of independent directors. Indeed, board independence plays a significant role in emerging countries where mechanisms that control insiders' self-dealing are weak. Having independent directors in emerging country firms is not a recipe for success; independent directors of family firms show lower attendance levels than in nonfamily firms (Bianco, Ciavarella, and Signoretti 2015).

Summarizing, having more independent directors should (a) enable ties to other organizations/stakeholders, (b) decrease environmental uncertainty, (c) facilitate strategic change and risk-taking, (c) increase firm legitimacy, (d) have higher level of knowledge and advice available to the CEO, (e) have superior monitoring of management, and finally (f) improve performance in emerging country firms as long as the directors are truly independent in the context of family firms.

The percentage of independent board members in Mexico is 24, 27, and 28 percent for 2008, 2011, and 2016, respectively. This is quite low for global standards and stands just slightly above the minimum required by law: 25 percent.

International Experience

Directors with international experience tend to have more understanding of global markets and business practices and are more attuned to opportunities to compete globally. Accumulated knowledge about foreign markets is important in overcoming the "psychic distance" of doing business abroad. International experience could be a substitute for cultural knowledge, which is necessary for successfully formulating and implementing an international strategy.

International experience helps to reduce uncertainty and builds cultural knowledge within groups since it complements and expands other experiences. It also contributes to expand a firm's network that is critical to compete in the global environment. Thus, the international experience of a board provides the firm with resources like cultural knowledge, business and social networks, and global business expertise.

Board members with international experience can also complement the experience of top executives, which can be important in the advisory function that boards perform.

Board members with international experience in Mexico are 5, 8, and 6 percent for 2008, 2011, and 2016, respectively, which would seem low for a country that is a global leader in the number of free trade agreements it has in place.

Government Experience

Government policy can affect the competitive positions of firms by imposing taxes or altering firm costs through regulation. Firms are devoting increased attention and resources to a wide array of legislative activities whether through direct or indirect political lobbying activities or campaign contributions in order to eliminate threats and create opportunities.

Governments can also be a large customer for firms and so building ties that provide unofficial links to government entities makes good business sense. Prior research has found that political ties are related to firm performance, innovation, and the formation of foreign alliances (Siegel 2007; Wang and Chung 2013; You and Du 2012). Government experience on the board can reduce transaction costs of securing information about political decisions and provide preferential access to current government officials. It can also facilitate access to bank financing, reducing the cost of capital (Farinós Viñas, García Martin, Herrero Piqueras, and Ibáñez Escribano 2016).

It is possible that government officials influence results in industries where firms are more dependent on government decisions—*energy, infrastructure, defense.* We also believe that in large emerging economies (i.e., Mexico), the influence of government officials can have a broader effect on large foreign firms, blurring the boundaries among industries. In many emerging economies, privatization plans periodically take place on diverse industries and infrastructure projects.

Summarizing, we believe that boards with former government officials in emerging countries could contribute to higher performance because of the increased ability of the firm to co-opt foreign governments in their favor. This should decrease environmental uncertainty by decreasing regulatory pressures and gain greater access to critical information. Having said this, directors with government experience can also exacerbate problems of minority shareholder expropriations and so this attribute should be considered with care. Government experience in Mexico for 2008, 2011 and 2016 stands at 3, 6, and 4 percent of board members.

Education

General human capital is a skill that is valuable across industries and countries. Education is an attribute associated with general human capital since it reflects not only the information learned but also an individual's intelligence. The positive effect of education on organizational outcomes has been shown by previous research (Carpenter and Westphal 2001); directors with higher education have shown to have greater cognitive ability to contribute to an organization. Individuals with higher education are also able to find more creative solutions (Khanna, Jones, and Boivie 2014).

Board members' academic level determines their skills and knowledge level. The higher the education level, the more willingness to use external information, create networks, use external consultants, or monitor accounting systems (Crabtree and Gomolka 1991).

Directors with higher qualifications would extend group knowledge and stimulate other board members to consider different alternatives, increasing the capacity to process problems.

As a group, a board combines a mix of competencies and capabilities that jointly represent a pool of social capital and adds value in executing the board's governance function. Education level can be an influential factor for firm performance. Board members with higher educational qualifications will represent skills and competences as firms face demands for more sophisticated talent.

Board members with a higher level of education will also tend to be more independent minded in their decision making, confident that their educational background supports their choices. They might be more willing to suggest radical courses of action for the organization, since they are not so concerned about losing their jobs.

The institutional approach to corporate governance suggests that governance systems are affected by institutional differences. Not only board members' culture but also their education shapes their cognitive reasoning skills and decision-making process. Directors with a higher level of education should make more informed decisions.

Finally, higher educational level is associated with innovation receptivity, tolerance for ambiguity, and the assimilation of large amounts of complex information (Goll, Johnson, and Rasheed 2007). A primary contributor to the legitimacy of CEOs and directors is human capital.

The education level of board members in Mexico has remained stable over time; 70 percent of board members had a bachelor's degree, 28 percent a master's, and 2 percent a PhD in 2008. For 2016, those same figures were 64, 33, and 3, respectively.

Functional Background

We define functional background diversity as the range of predominant job function where directors have worked during their careers. This variable represents the range of skill sets and network resources available to a board.

Since individuals are drawn to functional areas that suit their personalities, we can say that individuals in different functions have different cognitive models. Indeed, functional background has been found to significantly influence executives' analytical and decision-making perspectives (Wiersema and Bantel 1992). This is probably because with time, individuals tend to adhere to their professional areas' code of thinking. Therefore, managers will probably prefer information that fits their functional backgrounds. CEOs and board members with similar backgrounds develop common belief structures that prompt them to diagnose strategic issues analogously and to prefer similar solutions (Walsh 1988; Hambrick and Mason 1984).

Groups with a broader functional background will be better able to deal with environmental complexities (Finkelstein, Hambrick, and Cannella 2008). Boards with a more diverse set of backgrounds will benefit from the breadth of knowledge, perspectives, experiences, capabilities, and values that are represented within different fields of expertise. Further, a wider set of experiences and perspectives should lead to better and more thorough evaluation of alternatives to creatively solve complex problems, reduce groupthink, and increase the quality of decisions (Doz and Kosonen 2007).

Hambrick and Mason (1984) divided functional background in three categories: "output," "throughput," and "peripheral" functions. The "output" functions include functional areas related to merchandising, marketing, and sales as well as product research, development, and entrepreneurship. "Throughput" functions include engineering, process engineering, and production/operations, which intend to increase the efficiency in the transformation process. Finally, "peripheral" functions are law and finance.

Executives with "output" background tend to have greater ambiguity and less control, whereas those with "throughput" and "peripheral" background tend more to control (Hermann and Datta 2002). "Throughput" backgrounds are important in industries that are characterized by high capital intensity or concentration and lower growth. Hambrick and Mason (1984) propose that "output" functional experience of top managers would positively relate to profitability and growth in turbulent industries with observable differences, while "throughput" functional experience would be more effective in stable industries. Functional background has also been associated with selective perception in areas where the manager has a high level of competence. For example, a director with functional experience from research and development is more likely to perceive changes in competitors' product designs than does a manager with a functional background in sales and marketing. Board members with formal education in the sciences or with a specialty in an engineering-related field have a better understanding of technology advancements and, therefore, encourage cooperative and innovative opportunities.

Overall, research evidence suggests that functional background diversity is likely to stimulate task conflict and to improve performance (Pelled, Eisenhardt, and Xin 1999).

In Mexico, 51, 8, and 41 percent had backgrounds in throughput (engineering, operations, accounting), output (marketing, sales), and peripheral (law and finance), respectively. For 2011, the measures were similar: 50, 5, and 44 percent for throughput, output, and peripheral. There is no available data for 2016.

Firm Age

Average firm age for Mexican firms stands at 38.5 years. The average age of a US S&P 500 firm is under 20 years when in the 1950s it was 60 years (Credit Suisse 2017). This is probably a signal that Mexico needs both a higher number of new public firms and related to this more firms in high-tech sectors.

Industry

We classified industry types according to the North American Industry Classification System (NAICS). Firms in the sample remain pretty stable as can be observed in Table 6.2. The only significant change in the three measured periods is in the mining, utilities, and construction sector, which went from 25 to 29 and finally 30 percent of firms in the sample.

Table 6.1 Board member variables

Variable	Scale	2008			2011			2016		
		Min	Max	Avg.	Min	Max	Avg.	Min	Max	Avg.
Foreigners (%)	Binomial	0	1	8.00%	0	1	10%	0	1	12.12%
Women	Binomial	0	0	0.00%	0	1	5.1%	1	0	7.6%
Age	Years	28	84	0.00	26	90	90	21	90	56.65
Tenure	Years	0	67	0.00	0	58	10.74	0	54	10.61
Duality	Binomial	0	0%	38.00%	0	0%	37.00%	0	1%	44.00%
Independence	% Board Members	0	0	24.00%	0	1%	2.99%	0	1%	2.05%
International Experience	% Board Members	0.0%	58.0%	5.0%	0.0%	71.0%	8.0%	0.0%	52.0%	6.0%
Government Experience	% Board Members	0.0%	58.0%	3.0%	0.0%	64.0%	6.0%	0.0%	57.0%	4.0%
Education	Range	1	5	1.71	1	5	1.73	1	5	1.96
BA	% Board Members	5%	100%	70%	4%	100%	64%	14%	100%	64%
MA	% Board Members	2%	92%	16%	4%	100%	19%	3%	73%	13%
MBA	% Board Members	4%	65%	12%	4%	64%	14%	5%	76%	20%
PhD	% Board Members	2%	19%	2%	2%	43%	3%	3%	32%	3%
Functional Background										
Throughput	% Board Members	0%	90%	49%	0%	100%	44%	0%	55%	19%
Output	% Board Members	0%	38%	6%	0%	33%	5%	0%	42%	7%
Peripheral	% Board Members	10%	100%	44%	0%	100%	48%	0%	67%	33%
Financial Experts	% Board Members	0%	50%	9%	0%	42%	12%	0%	71%	34%
Total sample, N=79										

Source: Rivas, J.L., and J. Rubio. 2018. "Boards & TMTs in Mexico." Working Paper.

Reputation

Reputation revolves around a firm being "known for something" (Lange, Lee, and Dai 2010). The idea of reputation as "perceived quality" (Rindova et al. 2005, p. 1035) refers to the firm's ability to create value consistently in a way that is positively assessed by stakeholders. Reputation is an asset and can be considered an essential element of firm competitive advantage.

Firm reputation is important for its growth and survival. Trust and confidence of consumers can influence firm profitability. In the past decade, the importance of reputation has increasingly gained influence probably due to the networked world where consumers can learn in real time about product failures in faraway countries and regions, hence the importance for businesses to respond fast to crises that may question their reputation.

While it constitutes an intangible concept, a good reputation can benefit firms not only through buying preferences but also for consumer goodwill in times of crises.

Firm reputation allows product differentiation in highly competitive markets and premium pricing and can be the most important attribute that a consumer uses to decide among competing products and services.

The reputation of a business depends on different features: one is consistency in delivering on promises to customers and vendors. A second one is being transparent and responsive.

A third feature of a good reputation is how employees perceive their workplace: if they are around talented colleagues, feel well treated, and find the firm an appealing place to work, learn, and grow.

We will use this component as a proxy of firm reputation by providing evidence of the number of firms that are listed in the "Great Place to Work" list that is published every year.

Our database only has data for one year—2012—and we can see that only 14 percent of firms were included in the ranking.

Number of Committees

Committees allow the board to divide its work among directors; they also allow board members to develop specialized knowledge about specific issues. Henke (1986) argued that the board's primary influence on strategy is through its committees.

In the United States, public company boards are required to have independent audit, nominating–governance, as well as compensation committees. Additionally, a growing number of firms are creating other types of board committees to analyze the concerns of external stakeholders. These committees are usually called public responsibility, corporate social responsibility, stakeholder relations, or external affairs committees (De Kluyver 2009).

Two factors in the past decade have combined to make board committees much more important; the first is the substantial increase in litigations against independent directors. This has made it more difficult for firms to recruit independent directors due to the exposure of potential lawsuits. The second factor is the implementation of the Sarbanes–Oxley Act in 2002. Among other issues, this act requires that firms have audit committees that include a financial expert. In 2002, the New York Stock Exchange (NYSE) amended its own rules to mandate that the boards of all NYSE firms include compensation, nominating, and audit committees made up entirely of independent directors.

Due to the recentness of these changes, there is limited empirical evidence pointing to the effectiveness of board committees; Eminet and Guedri (2010) do show how nominating committees can reduce the influence of CEOs on new directors' appointments. In a sample of Spanish firms, García-Sánchez (2010) found a positive relationship between business technical efficiency and a higher number of board committees. Thus, we need more empirical evidence to conclude on the effectiveness of board committees.

In Mexico, securities law requires public firms to have a minimum of two board committees: audit and legal. Both committees should be made only of independent nonaffiliated directors with a minimum of three individuals in each committee.

The number of board committees in our sample went from 2.5 to 2.9 and back to 2.5 in 2008, 2011, and 2016, respectively. This means that on average Mexican public firms have 20 percent more committees than what the law requires, which probably means that most firms do not see in board committees a vehicle to improve corporate governance.

These numbers could also be signaling a low commitment of government agencies to enforce regulations.

Board Evaluation

Boards must be concerned with more than organizational and management performance: they also need to review their own performance. In the past years, formal board evaluations have been increasingly used as a method of assessing the performance of boards of organizations due in part to increasing regulatory prescription.

Board evaluation can enhance board effectiveness and improve financial performance (Minichilli, Gabrielsson, and Huse 2007). Board evaluation is a good way for boards to show they are serious about their performance and that they are willing to expose themselves to the same type of processes that managers go through setting an organizational example.

Board evaluations help establish the individual and collective responsibilities of directors and identify where the board as a whole and the individual directors need to change. Evaluations allow boards to diagnose areas of concern and to identify sources of failure, translating findings into a comprehensive action plan of change.

Board evaluations confer legitimacy to a board by decreasing their dependence from the CEO and the TMT. Additionally, board evaluations contribute to improve board processes and higher qualified directors.

The number of firms with board evaluation processes has improved; it grew from 57 to 70 and then to 75 percent in 2008, 2011, and 2016, respectively.

Board Meetings

Board meetings are an important source of information for directors; more meetings mean more opportunities to obtain relevant information that will allow them to be more effective.

Board meetings are used as a measure of intensity of board activity. The effectiveness of a board partially depends on how often the board members meet to discuss the issues addressing a firm. Diligent boards will increase the level of supervision, resulting in improved firm performance.

In addition to board meetings, board diligence comprises other aspects such as attentiveness during meetings, preparation, participation, and postmeeting follow-up.

Board meetings provide benefits like more time for directors to discuss, set strategy, and monitor management, but it is also a fact that these meetings have associated costs such as managerial time, travel expense, and directors' fees.

Prior research suggests that a key impediment to board effectiveness is a lack of time to complete board duties. Hence, the more time the board spends together discussing firm issues, the more likely it is to perform their duties diligently and in accordance with shareholder interests (Lipton and Lorsch 1992). If meetings allow enough time for board members to discuss and understand in detail the operation and needs of the firm, the decision-making process will eventually be easier and take less time.

The number of board meetings in our sample has remained pretty stable. It was 3.9 meetings per year in 2008 and then went to 4 both for 2011 and 2016. This is low when compared to international standards; at S&P 500 firms, the average number of meetings is twice that of our sample (8.2). Again, like with board committees, it is significant that the figure in our sample is just what the law requires (4). This leads us to believe that board meetings are probably not perceived as a tool to improve corporate governance.

Firm Internationalization

Internationalization is a potential strategy increasingly used by business firms to learn, grow revenue, increase profitability and market share, and to eventually become an industry leader. It is an important attribute of many current strategy processes in the business world. Becoming an international firm carries serious changes in values, scope, principles, action orientation, nature of work, norms, and business regulations. The internationalization dimension is related to all these aspects of the strategy process and can transform a firm into "Transnational." In the global marketplace, it is important to become a transnational. An internationalization process emphasizes firm development on the acquisition, integration, and use of knowledge about foreign markets and operations.

Globalization of the market is one of the most significant changes in work environment over the last decades. Long-term success and survival increasingly depend on having a strong international presence (Barkema and Vermeulen 1998). Global activities will increase firm complexity; the range of cultures, customers, and competitors will probably grow as a firm internationalizes. But globalization also provides opportunities for growth in the form of scale—scope economies and learning. Internationalization enables firms to leverage R&D costs and knowledge across countries and respond to foreign competitors in a domestic market.

Firm internationalization in our sample is measured in two ways: foreign sales and foreign assets. We do this since a firm might excel in being an international marketer but not really have much investments overseas. Foreign assets are a measure of how much "skin in the game" a firm has abroad. Our results show that the internationalization of Mexican public firms has improved significantly using either one of our proxies: with foreign sales the figure increases from 8 to 11 and then to 21 percent in 2008, 2011, and 2016, respectively. Foreign assets increase from 14 to 8 and to 21 percent for those same three years.

Listed Foreign Exchanges

Firms with access to foreign capital markets have easier access to capital. Thus, they have an incentive to implement sound governance practices. Other than more favorable terms for capital, firms also list in stronger institutional environments in order to commit to tougher disclosure and corporate governance rules in what has been termed "bonding." Doidge et al. (2009) show how controlling shareholders that consume higher private benefits of control are more reluctant to list their shares on a US exchange despite the financing benefits. Silvers and Elgers (2015) report that bonding is an important factor to increase the valuation of non-US firms.

The percentage of firms listed in foreign exchanges has remained stable for our measured period; it was 25 percent in 2008 and then 27 percent for both 2011 and 2016.

Table 6.2 Firm variables

Variable	Scale	2008			2011			2016		
		Min	Max	Avg.	Min	Max	Avg.	Min	Max	Avg.
Year Found	Years	1925.00	2015.00	1979.47	-	-	-	-	-	-
Industry (NAICS)		-	-	-	-	-	-	-	-	-
Food	%	-	-	15%	-	-	15%	-	-	15%
Mining, Ut, and Construction	%	-	-	25%	-	-	29%	-	-	30%
Trade and Transportation	%	-	-	8%	-	-	9%	-	-	9%
Prof and Info Services	%	-	-	1%	-	-	1%	-	-	1%
Manufacturing	%	-	-	6%	-	-	6%	-	-	6%
Other Services	%	-	-	33%	-	-	38%	-	-	38%
Reputation 2012	0%	-	-	-	-	-	-	-	-	-
				68%			68%			68%
	1%			14%			14%			14%
Number of Committees		1.00	8.00	2.58	1	7.00	2.91	1.00	6	2.55
Board Evaluation	%	0%		57%	0%		70%	0%		75%
Foreign Sales/Total Sales	%	0%	75%	8%	0%	82%	11%	0%	83%	21%
Foreign Assets/Total Assets	%			14.00			8.00			21.00
Listed Foreign Exchange	%			25%			27%			27%
Board Meetings	Nominal	0.00	7.00	3.91	4.00	6.00	4.08	0.00	12.00	4.09
Foreign Assets/Total Assets	%			14.00			8.00			21.00
Listed Foreign Exchange	%			25%			27%			27%
Board Meetings	Nominal	0.00	7.00	3.91	4.00	6.00	4.08	0.00	12.00	4.09
Total sample, N=79.										

Source: Rivas, J.L., and J. Rubio. 2018. "Boards & TMTs in Mexico." Working Paper.

CHAPTER 7

Corporate Networks in Mexico

Corporate networks are the foreseeable links between companies and their leaders. They are formed by ties among directors sitting in more than one board—*interlocks*. These links are proxies of a country's economic structure and its corporate governance system. Because economic action is embedded in social structures (Granovetter 1985), individuals are actors operating within a network. Individuals then can not only influence these networks but they are also constrained by them.

Networks emerge because boards are made of insiders and outsiders. Outsiders are usually recruited from other firms or from financial, public, or government institutions. This recruitment is many times based on shared backgrounds, friendship, or family ties (Scott 1991). Directors with more than three board positions are known as "big linkers" and they are considered an inner circle of the business elite, which can be politically influential and usually defend the interests of the business elite.

Differences in institutional backgrounds can lead to different developments of corporate networks across countries. The "cultural and historical embeddedness of personal, capital and commercial relations in business" (Scott 1991, 1995) deeply influences networks; Mexico experienced long periods of instability after independence from Spain in 1821. Stability prevailed for 34 years with the dictatorship of Porfirio Diaz (1876 to 1910) but then relapsed with the Mexican revolution (1910 to 1927). Political instability usually leads to weaker institutions: Maurer and Sharma (2001) suggest that poor protection of property rights in Mexico is a key reason for the existence of corporate elites. Because collateral was hard to repossess in a default case, banks and firms developed business groups to function as monitors and contract enforcers. Haber, Razo, and Maurer

(2003) argue that to overcome poor property rights protection, the government and the elites developed an implicit regulatory pact where they became partners in the distribution of privileges and rents while guaranteeing enforcement of these rights to select groups. Personal elite connections were also necessary to get equity buyers or bank loans. Hence, firms in Mexico probably relied on networks to substitute for the country's institutional failures (Musacchio and Read 2007).

In 1982 the Mexican banking system was nationalized; this event altered the country's network structure since banks and business groups had developed intense relationships. Banks were privatized in 1989, reestablishing the network centralized structure. The Mexican financial crisis of 1994 altered the network structure again: after the crisis, foreign ownership of banks increased to more than 90 percent and the network experienced less interaction intensity as well as dispersion and withdrawal. This was probably because the network was losing significance both for domestic and foreign members. This last event proved more harmful for the network's interlocking patterns than the 1982 nationalization (Salas-Porras 2006a).

Today, interlocking directorates are still commonplace in Mexico: not only within business groups but across them. This allows controlling shareholders to exercise a greater influence over firms. Independent directors are many times chosen on the basis of loyalty and personal relationships rather than on technical skills or unbiased views.

Because networks have proved to be a substitute for formal institutions, firm owners still use them to monitor each other negotiating in a system that relies more on traditions. Large shareholders also assume board positions to protect their investments and link their firms (Auvray and Brossard 2013). Countries dominated by business groups (i.e., Taiwan) show that board interlocks are primarily used as control mechanisms (Brookfield 2010). Thus, countries with high ownership concentration tend to have more interlocks and cohesive corporate networks. Cohesive networks also allow for collusion, collaboration, cooperation, and collective action, while fragmented networks foster autonomy, competition, and reduce contagion risks (Mizruchi 1996; Cárdenas 2014).

Musacchio and Read (2007) conclude that in Mexico: i) there are a large number of connections due to directors serving in various boards simultaneously and ii) politicians play a more important role in the network. In a more recent study that compares networks in Latin America, Cárdenas (2016) concludes that in countries where state–business relationships are moderated by strong business associations (i.e., Mexican CMN/CCE) and are open to free trade with developed economies, corporate elites form cohesive networks (Mexico, Chile). And in countries where business associations are weak, state–business relationships are particularistic, and domestic markets are protected from foreign competition—*Brasil, Colombia*—corporate elites do not feel the need to form cohesive networks.

In Tables 7.1, 7.2, and 7.3 we can see the main characteristics of the most central directors (1900 to 2015) and firms (2015). Please note how the importance of government ties decreases significantly in the two periods; in 1900 only two of the most central individuals were not tied to the government. In 2015 it is the opposite; only two of the most central individuals had government ties. It is also interesting to note that these two individuals had "technical" and not "political" ties to the government: Jaime Serra-Puche was secretary of commerce when NAFTA was negotiated and Everardo Elizondo was deputy governor for the Bank of Mexico.

Table 7.1 Most central directors 1900

Name	Position
1. Pablo Macedo	Lawyer and Congressman
2. Guillermo Landa y Escandon	Senator
3. Hugo Scherer	Member of Banking Commission
4. Ernesto Brown	N.A.
5. Luis Elguero	Lawyer; Mayor, Mexico City
6. Fernando Pimentel y Fagoaga	Mayor, Mexico City; Member of Banking & Monetary commission
7. Jose Signoret	Lawyer and Congressman
8. Enrique Creel	Congressman; Ambassador of Mexico in the United States; Minister of Foreign Affairs
9. Luis Riba	Financier
10. Carlos Casaus	Congressman for the State of Mexico

Source: Based on Eigen centrality. Musacchio, A., and I. Read. 2007. "Bankers, Industrialists, and their Cliques: Elite Networks in Mexico and Brazil during Early Industrialization." *Enterprise & Society* 8, no. 4, pp. 842-80.

Table 7.2 Most central directors 2015

Name	Position
1. Alfonso Gonzalez Migoya	Chairman, Volaris
2. Valentin Diez Morodo	Chairman, Citi Banamex
3. Jaime Serra-Puche	Chairman, SAI Consulting
4. Claudio X Gonzalez	Chairman, Kimberly Clark
5. Alfredo Livas Cantu	Chairman, Praxis Finance
6. Everardo Elizondo Almaguer	Deputy Governor, Bank of Mexico
7. Eduardo Tricio Haro	Chairman, Grupo Lala
8. Carlos Salazar Lomelin	CEO, Femsa
9. Alvaro Fernandez Garza	Chairman and CEO, Alfa
10. Armando Garza Sada	Former Chairman, Alfa

Source: Based on Eigen centrality. Salvaj, E., J.L. Rivas, and M. Cordova. 2018. "Corporate Elites in Latin America." Working Paper.

Table 7.3 Most central firms 2015

Firm	Industry
1. Kimberly Clark	Consumer products
2. Cydsasa	Chemical
3. Nemak	Autoparts
4. Liverpool	Retail; Department Stores
5. Palacio de Hierro	Retail; Department Stores
6. Banorte	Financial Services
7. Axtel	Telecommunications
8. Cemex	Materials; Cement
9. Bolsa Mexicana de Valores	Financial Services
10. Peñoles	Materials; Mining

Source: Based on Eigen centrality. Salvaj, E., J.L. Rivas, and M. Cordova. 2018. "Corporate Elites in Latin America." Working Paper.

CHAPTER 8

An Interview with Jaime Serra-Puche

Jaime is the most central independent director of listed firms in Mexico for 2015. Centrality is determined by the number of directorships on boards with high connectivity. Jaime is currently the Chairman of BBVA Bancomer, the country's largest financial institution. He is also a director at: Tenaris, Vitro, Fondo Mexico. In the past he has held directorships at Chiquita (United States), Grupo Ferroviario Mexicano, Grupo Modelo, Southern Peru Copper, Rotoplas, Fresnillo, and Alpek.

He holds a BA in political science from UNAM, a master's in economics from Colegio de Mexico, and a PhD in economics from Yale. He was deputy secretary of the treasury, secretary of the treasury, secretary of trade and industry, and is currently chairman of SAI Consulting. Jaime is probably best known as Mexico's chief negotiator for NAFTA.

- *How do you compare being a board member in the United States versus in Mexico?*
  a. Who is in charge: in the United States the board is really in charge of crucial decisions.
  b. Diligence: a director in Mexico does not invest a lot of time to prepare for a board meeting. In the United States, you are expected to prepare and study for each meeting.
  c. Rigor: there is more consistency in the United States regarding fiduciary duty and the time you devote to a board. In Mexico, that same fiduciary duty exists but directors devote less time to board work.

- *What are the main obstacles for improving corporate governance in Mexico?*

  a. Roles: top managers in Mexico see the board as a formality and not as a potential contributor to their performance. Projects presented at board meetings are already processed and boards are expected to approve them. In the United States, a board usually works with top managers to improve their projects before they are approved.

  b. Attributes: directors in Mexico tend to be older males with more social affinity to their peers. Average tenure of directors is also longer, with fewer age or tenure limits to service.

  c. Information access: the level and depth of information available to directors in Mexico is low. This is partially a consequence of not only our weak institutional environment but also strategic avoidance schemes where controlling shareholders prefer to control agendas.

  d. Ownership concentration. Mexico has high levels of ownership concentration and average firm age is high. Hence, controlling shareholders do not have enough incentives to use their boards as vehicles for change. Most firms feel successful with their status quo. Many family firms become public but only modify their governance to comply with regulation. The main motivation of family firms to become public is to facilitate succession.

- *How can corporate governance improve in Mexico?*

  a. CEO succession plans are almost nonexistent in Mexico and in other countries it is a regulatory requirement. Cemex is one of the few firms that have them in place and that is why when Lorenzo Zambrano died their stock price did not suffer much.

  b. Board and CEO evaluation need to be performed periodically and in a consistent manner. As we speak, they only take place episodically.

  c. Regulation: there is room for improvement. Policy makers can incentivize the presence of foreign institutional investors as block holders. They could also impose stricter regulations on dual class shares and pyramidal structures than inhibit the one share–one vote principle.

d. Culture: the value of regulation has not permeated. Firms comply with governance regulations as if they were just requirements. They do not adhere to the "spirit" of these norms. Within boards, there is little value placed on board debate. The ideas that can be generated through discussions with independent board members do not seem to be attractive for managers or controlling shareholders. Relationships between controlling shareholders and independent directors tend to be personal and this inhibits director accountability. When a controlling shareholder invites an independent director to join a board it is difficult to establish a frank dialogue as to what is expected...and there should be one, because if there is none then a sense of "collusion" can remain in the relationship and it becomes hard for that independent member to debate with the people that invited him/her. Independent board members, therefore, need to improve their understanding of what it means to be "independent" from the moment they are invited to join; they are supposed to represent minority—*and not majority*—shareholders and this issue should be in the first conversations with whomever invites them to join a board. Of course, this can be uncomfortable but is certainly necessary. On the other hand, majority owners also need to appreciate the value that independent mentalities bring to the table...not just in open board discussions but in board committees and evaluation processes.

e. Inequality: Mexican society is hierarchical and highly unequal so the idea of directors as members of a "small world" often takes place, and this contributes to perpetuate differences that society as a whole must try to overcome. We need more "new economy" firms in our stock exchange. This should help to modernize director mentalities and roles.

    f. Board diligence systems: I have worked on this quite a bit now that I am serving as chairman at BBVA. These systems are prevalent in many US boards and they help board members be better prepared for meetings. They are safe encrypted software programs where directors can see—*and not print*—the materials related to future meetings.

    g. Executive sessions only for independent members. This is still a rarity in Mexico because owners feel uncomfortable with them....but they are certainly necessary to improve the quality of independence in most boards.

- *Can you share one or two of your most difficult moments as a director?*

One of them took place while serving at the Chiquita board in the United States. We were paying "security fees" to a guerrilla group so that our banana farmers could work. This group eventually joined the governmental list of terrorist groups but Chiquita only learned this afterward and, as a consequence, we gained a serious legal liability with the US government. As an independent board member, I pushed the board for voluntary disclosure. The board agreed and even though it was voluntary, our reputation and stock price decreased. We had to pay over US$100 million in legal fees and penalties over several years to solve this issue.

A second difficult issue happened at a large Mexican firm where independent board members had to become referees of a serious problem between two of the firm's controlling families. We were able to avoid litigation and eventually convinced both parties to recruit professional talent to manage the firm.

CHAPTER 9

An Interview with Claudio X Gonzalez

Don Claudio—*as he is known*—is a good example of a director who has become a very central independent director among large Mexican firms. His views are complementary to Jaime Serra's in that he is well known as an "owner." Jaime is known as a "professional outsider."

Don Claudio is currently the chairman of Kimberly Clark Mexico and serves on the boards of: Fondo Mexico, Grupo Alfa, Grupo Carso, Grupo Mexico, Salzburg Global Seminar, and the Baker Institute for Public Policy. He is also an advisor to Capital Group and an emeritus director at GE.

He holds a chemical engineering degree from Stanford and is a graduate from the Mexican Institute for Business Administration. He has represented the interests of Mexican businesses as president of the Consejo Mexicano de Negocios, Consejo Coordinador Empresarial—*equivalent to US Business Roundtable*—and the Centro de Estudios Económicos del Sector Privado—*a think tank funded by the private sector.*

- *What are the main obstacles for improving corporate governance in Mexico?*
    a. There is a large amount of family ownership that makes this more difficult. Family ownership will be dispersed when the country is able to achieve high sustained economic growth.
    b. Unwillingness to be open; many firms are still "secretive." They do not want to be listed because this would mean opening up to scrutiny.

    c. Lack of diversity; Mexico is still homogeneous regarding board composition. This is partially due to the unavailability of a diverse talent pool of candidates.

- *How can corporate governance be improved?*
  a. By having more listed firms; we can achieve this by growing more aggressively. If a firm needs capital to grow it will be more likely to go public and improve governance standards in order to more diligently respond to stakeholder interests.
  b. Raising the awareness of the corporate governance topic. More research is needed.

- *Can you share one or two of your most difficult moments as a director?*

As a GE director during the 2008 financial crisis. GE Capital was the sixth largest financial institution in the United States and it was very close to bankruptcy because the markets for short-term capital were not going to open on a Monday and the firm needed to refinance its debt holdings. The issue was solved through a bridge loan from the New York Federal Reserve at the last minute, but these were tough times for those of us serving on the Board and Audit Committees.

CHAPTER 10

Suggestions to Move Forward

Despite changes in corporate law and the introduction of the code, ownership of Mexican public firms is still heavily concentrated and this presents incentives that harm the three principals of good governance: transparency, balance of power, and accountability. Having said this, we also need to acknowledge the increasing importance of private equity and institutional investment among the newer public firms. The presence of this type of block holders should improve the quality of governance due to an increase in accountability and power balance. The caveat here is that the number of firms that go public in Mexico is low even for emerging markets; according to Rivas and Adamuz (2017), in a study using 63 developed and emerging countries Mexico ranks 48th in terms of IPOs/population during 2001 to 2014. Among the large emerging economies that fare better than Mexico are China, Chile, Croatia, Turkey, Brazil, Indonesia, Philippines, South Africa, India, and Russia.

The presence of women directors in our sampled firms is remarkably low (6 percent: Table 6.1) not only for social responsibility reasons but also for informed decision making at the board level; women take buying decisions of many kinds of products so firms need a minimum quota of gender representatives both at the board and TMTs. An average of 6 percent (Table 6.1) of international experience is low for a country with the size of trade that Mexico has. Diversity can have positive effects on board performance. A growing body of research suggests that board member diversity brings unique perspectives to boards and contributes to build social capital (e.g., Arfken, Bellar, and Helms 2004; Rivas 2012b).

Diversity can also enhance a board's independence of thought (Adams and Ferreira 2009). Other specific areas to improve include:

A) Committees. By having, on average, a number slightly above legal requirements (2), it could be that committees in Mexico are seen more as a bureaucratic procedure rather than a vehicle for improving governance quality. If, for example, a firm is committed to improve the legitimacy of its independence level, a nomination committee that recruits, evaluates, and proposes candidates for the board is destined to play a pivotal role (EY-ICSA 2016).

B) Training. This is a recommendation that comes from a Deloitte 2018 survey of board members. New members need to learn not only about their board duties but also about the businesses that the firm does. An ideal training for board members could then include meetings with clients, suppliers, top managers, and facility inspections.

C) Tenure. According to Granovetter (1985), human beings are not only rational and self-interested actors that make decisions independently of others. Rather, we are all embedded in relationships that inform our decisions so it is harder to remain independent as time passes. It is true that relationships do not determine individual actions but they do inform and add value to them through the transfer of fine-grained information, trust and joint problem solving. Hence, serving time of board members should not exceed a limit. In our analysis we find that this figure is high: average tenure at S&P firms is 8.2 years (Spencer Stuart 2017) versus 10.7 years for Mexico. An avenue to decrease it could include a retirement age policy. Among Fortune 100 firms, 72 years is the norm (EY 2015).

D) Board evaluations have grown in importance (from 57 percent in 2008 to 75 percent in 2016). Most annual reports do not disclose the type or period where they were performed. Anecdotal evidence points to these assessments as being performed on an irregular and sometimes informal basis. According to the OECD Board evaluation report (2018), It is recommended that they are done periodically, comprehensively, supervised by a specific individual or board committee and disclosed in a formal manner in order to increase their potential contribution to governance effectiveness.

E) CEO and TMT succession plans. As with board training, this constitutes an area of opportunity; sixty-two percent of surveyed firms do not have one in place. Compensation procedures for top managers and board committees are also needed (Deloitte 2013). These processes could potentially be a task for a compensation/human capital board committee.

F) Increase in transparency of top-level compensation and nomination practices. According to the CFA Corporate Governance Manual (2018), the disclosure of executive pay sheds light on a board's stewardship of firm assets. This disclosure allows investors to assess whether compensation practices are reasonable in light of their reported performance. One way to implement this could be using an independent board committee (compensation/human capital/nomination) that designs and proposes for board approval a system of TMT - board compensation and recruitment. A simplified version—for clarity purposes—could then be disclosed to shareholders in the annual report - meeting.

G) Duality. CEO duality occurs when the same person holds the CEO and chair roles. In stable periods, independence between the chairman and CEO roles contributes to improved accountability in the boardroom since the board is expected to monitor top managers. It has been argued that if the CEO also chairs the board, there might be a conflict of interest in the board's monitoring of the TMT (Monks and Minow 2008). Duality is in fact forbidden by law in the United Kingdom but it is a widespread phenomenon in Mexico where 44 percent of firms exhibited this trait in 2016. Research has shown, however, that duality can help to overcome crisis faster; CEO duality becomes beneficial as concentrated power allows the firm to respond more rapidly to a crisis (Dowell, Shackell, and Stuart 2011). But, in contexts with low institutional quality and financial market development, CEO duality could deter firm performance (Mutlu et al. 2017). Thus, given the above-mentioned arguments CEO duality should be evaluated carefully.

H) Functional background diversity. A diverse board is less susceptible to "groupthink" (Barkema and Vermeulen 1998). Although it is related to task conflict, it improves performance on cognitive tasks (Jehn, Northcarft, and Neale 1997). Functionally diverse teams may be better linked into external networks, allowing them greater access to information (Milliken and Martins 1996). One way to increase diversity could be setting quotas for the most important background profiles -*finance, operations, production, and technical*- these quotas could also be aligned with corporate objectives such as entering a new country or industry.

I) Age. Firms could try to better match board entrants so that there are "cohorts" of director age. Setting limits to tenure and establishing a retirement age could aid a process of achieving board age diversity. Hacksoon and Chanwoo (2010) found that age diversity at the board level positively affects firm valuation. On the other hand, groups characterized by diversity in age may find it difficult to communicate, conflict is more likely, and social integration harder to achieve. A younger board takes more risk, innovates more, and has higher levels of energy (Barker and Mueller 2002).

J) Meetings. Boards in Mexico hold the number of meetings that are legally required (4). Many strategic decisions are made during board meetings. It is true that a board should avoid implementing strategies and a high number of yearly meetings could be a signal of this behavior. As mentioned earlier, for S&P 500 firms in the US, the average is 8.2 meetings, which is more than double the Mexican average of 4. This lower result could be related to the high ownership concentration and low level of board independence exhibited in the country. Thus, it is possible that several boards in our sample could be acting more in an advisory than in a fiduciary role and, because of the oligopolistic nature of Mexican markets (COFECE 2018) where firms are able to charge premium prices due to their market dominance, controlling shareholders could feel that a board adds limited value to firm performance.

Overall, corporate governance practices in Mexico compare to those of OECD countries but fare below its average. Thus, we can conclude that Mexico needs to improve its governance practices if it truly aspires to become a developed economy or even a leader of emerging country practices.

A key regulatory issue that Mexico needs to address is the update of the Law of Mercantile Societies from 1934 so that it is consistent with the 2005 law of security markets. Most countries from the civil law tradition had this same problem but have managed to address it in recent years. Among those countries are Spain, Italy, Brazil, Colombia, and Chile. Until this matter is resolved, private firms in Mexico will not be required to have a board that follows global best practices. Hence, the regulatory framework in Mexico needs to be consistent in order for corporate governance best legal practices to permeate and contribute to improvements.

Because of the high level of ownership concentration, regulators should consider restricting pyramidal structures and the issuance of shares with restricted voting rights (currently at a threshold of 25 percent). Why? Because freely allowing this exacerbates the problem of control by few and ownership by many. Policy makers should consider that restricted voting rights create principal–agent problems where the principal (owner) is not able to exercise part of his/her rights and the agent (CEO) can distinguish between a "first" and "second" class of firm owners. A one share–one vote policy has been a practice consistent with sound corporate governance practices. Hence, regulators should reconsider the existing forms of equity issuance and decide if they enhance corporate governance practices.

Following the study of Machuga and Teitel (2009), policy makers should also consider redefining board independence to make it more rigorous and establishing a maximum number of directorships an individual board member can hold. Substitute board members is also a practice in Mexico that should be forbidden. Even if a substitute board member is as capable as the regular one, how can they follow pending issues that have been discussed in previous meetings? How can he/she earn minority shareholders' trust?

Babatz-Torres (1997) argues that Mexican law protects minority shareholders on the surface but needs to be much more specific to serve their interests against potential lawsuits from majority owners. Chong and López-de-Silanes (2007) mention that the country has reformed its securities laws but also agrees with the low degree of shareholder protection diagnosis.

As mentioned earlier, professionalizing board members would also help. Director institutes can play a key role in expanding the pool of competent candidates from which to select directors. This has proved to be a valuable resource in Brazil with the Brazilian Institute of Corporate Governance (IBGC) that was formed as a nonprofit organization in 1995 to improve the quality of directors and governance practices.

Private dispute resolution procedures are currently being tested in the Sao Paulo Stock Exchange. These mechanism between firms and shareholders could be promoted by creating professional shareholder arbitration panels and persuading firms to include this resource in their by-laws.

Another potential best practice is to include a minimum of corporate governance standards for firms that wish to be eligible for pension fund/institutional investments. It requires that companies establish mechanisms to ensure the protection and equitable treatment of shareholders. This has been done in Colombia where it is probably too soon to find its results.

Mexican firms that aspire to improve their governance practices could also partner with institutional investors as evidence shows that their presence can be an effective remedy to principal–principal problems of expropriation in family-controlled firms, especially in the absence of a market for corporate control (Young et al. 2002; Agrawal and Knoeber 1996).

In our results from the Expansion 500 data, we show that the highest performing group in terms of ROE are multinational subsidiaries (18 percent) followed by state-owned entities (13 percent) and domestic firms (9 percent). Because most domestic firms are family firms, our results could be suggesting that most family firms would indeed benefit from limiting family interaction to ownership and board representation as argued by Bennedsen, Pérez-González, and Wolfenzon (2010). Successful family firms then need to become experts in corporate governance, fully assuming their ownership responsibilities. Family executives should be the exception and not the norm among family firms. Good corporate governance principles should clearly establish the requisites for family members to become executives in the firm.

Finally, we need to keep in mind that the quality of written law and regulation is only one side of the coin. Good corporate governance also relies on business practices, compliance, and enforcement. A key challenge for policy makers in Mexico is to improve the enforcement of the existing laws and—*where necessary*—improve laws and regulations.

Epilogue

As I finish writing this book in August of 2019 a new government came into power. Most people chose this regime because it was perceived as an "outsider" option. Corruption and insecurity in Mexico have grown to historical peaks and the incoming president promised to tackle both issues. These problems have been remediated in other countries by having a state that creates incentives for people to invest and innovate, guaranteeing property rights (Acemoglu and Robinson 2013). Chile, South Korea, and Singapore were once poor emerging countries that have rapidly evolved to an almost developed country status by strengthening their institutions and investing in innovation. The new Mexican government is introducing changes that instead of strengthening institutions can weaken them: they have capped salaries for all top levels of government at the equivalent of the new Mexican president's salary of US$5,273 per month, which ranks as the third lowest salary for a Latin American president (El Economista 2018). Most high ranking officers and technical members of government were above this level, and as a result, many of them have chosen to leave either as early retirees or to search for opportunities in the private sector. The new congress has also passed a law where the new anticorruption general attorney who was initially going to be independent will now respond to the president. They also want the National Energy Commission to respond to the energy secretary. "Lopez Obrador takes on Mexico's institutions" (Financial Times 2019) summarizes several of these issues.

Why is this important for boards? In Chapter 3 we discussed how institutions are an essential part of the perceived level of corporate governance among business executives in a country; if you can rely on a sound legal framework, your level of discomfort with having large block holders is not important. Thus, in emerging countries, it is much easier for an incoming president—*especially if they have a congress majority*—to change laws and regulations. Hence, if country institutions are weakened over the next few years, the only way that corporate boards in Mexico can increase their perceived effectiveness among their stakeholders is by filling the country "institutional voids" (Palepu and Khanna 1998): having more independent directors, committees, meetings, board and CEO evaluations. This is one of the reasons why board independence is related to performance only in emerging countries (Rivas and Villamil 2018) because firms need to build up internally the institutions that their context does not have.

Thank you so much for taking the time to read what I have to say.

Jose Luis Rivas

References

Acemoglu, D., and J.A. Robinson. 2013. *Why Nations Fail: The Origins of Power, Prosperity, and Poverty.* New York, NY: Crown Books.

Adams, R.B., and D. Ferreira. 2009. "Women in the Boardroom and their Impact on Governance and Performance." *Journal of Financial Economics* 94, no. 2, pp. 291–309.

Adams, R.B., A.N. Licht, and L. Sagiv. 2011. "Shareholders and stakeholders: How Do Directors Decide?" *Strategic Management Journal* 32, no. 12, pp. 1331–55.

Agrawal, A., and C.R. Knoeber. 1996. "Firm Performance and Mechanisms to Control Agency Problems between Managers and Shareholders." *Journal of Financial and Quantitative Analysis* 31, no. 3, pp. 377–97.

Aguilera, R., and W. Judge. 2014. *Who Will Guard the Guardians?* Ontario, Canada: Ivey Publishing.

Amason, A.C. 1996. "Distinguishing the Effects of Functional and Dysfunctional Conflict in Strategic Decision Making: Resolving a Paradox for Top Management Teams." *Academy of Management Journal* 39, pp. 123–48.

Anderson, R., S. Mansi, and D. Reeb. 2004. "Board Characteristics Accounting Report Integrity and the Cost of Debt." *Journal of Accounting and Economics* 37, pp. 315–42.

Anderson, R.C., and D.M. Reeb. 2003a. "Founding-family Ownership and Firm Performance: Evidence from the S&P 500." *The Journal of Finance* 58, no. 3, pp. 1301–28.

Anderson, R.C., and D.M. Reeb. 2003b. "Founding-family Ownership, Corporate Diversification, and Firm Leverage." *Journal of Law & Economics* 46, pp. 653–80.

Anderson, R.C., and D.M. Reeb. 2004. "Board Composition: Balancing Family Influence in S&P 500 firms." *Administrative Science Quarterly* 49, no. 2, pp. 209–37.

Andres, C. 2008. "Large Shareholders and Firm Performance—An Empirical Examination of Founding-Family Ownership." *Journal of Corporate Finance* 14, no. 4, pp. 431–45.

Arfken, D.E., S.L. Bellar, and M.M. Helms. 2004. "The Ultimate Glass Ceiling Revisited: The Presence of Women on Corporate Boards." *Journal of Business Ethics* 50, no, 2, pp. 177–86.

Auvray, T., and O. Brossard. 2013. "French Connection: Interlocking Directorates and the Ownership-control Nexus in an Insider Governance System." CEPN Working papers hal-00842582, HAL.

Azoury, N., and E. Bouri. 2015. "Principal–Principal Conflicts in Lebanese Unlisted Family Firms." *Journal of Management & Governance* 19, no. 2, pp. 461–93.

Babatz-Torres, G.B. 1997. *Ownership Structure, Capital Structure, and Investment in Emerging Markets: The Case of Mexico.* Cambridge, MA: Harvard University.

Bammens, Y., W. Voordeckers, and A. Van Gils. 2011. "Boards of Directors in Family Businesses: A Literature Review and Research Agenda." *International Journal of Management Reviews* 13, no. 2, pp. 134–52.

Barkema, H.G., and F. Vermeulen. 1998. "International Expansion through Start-up or Acquisition: A Learning Perspective." *Academy of Management Journal* 41, no. 1, pp. 7–26.

Barker, V.L., III, and G.C. Mueller. 2002. "CEO characteristics and firm R&D spending." *Management Science* 48, no. 6, pp. 782–801.

Bebczuk, R.N., A.L.C. da Silva, A.E. Chong, J.J. Cruces, U. Garay, M. González, ... & López-de-Silanes, F. 2007. "Investor Protection and Corporate Governance: Firm-level Evidence across Latin America." In *Latin American Development Forum Series.* Inter-American Development Bank.

Bennedsen, M., F. Pérez-González, and D. Wolfenzon. 2010. "The Governance of Family Firms." In *Corporate Governance: A Synthesis of Theory, Research, and Practice,* ed. K.H. Baker and R. Anderson. Hoboken, NJ: John Wiley & Sons, p. 8.

Bennedsen, M., K.M. Nielsen, F. Pérez-González, & D. Wolfenzon. 2007. "Inside the Family Firm: The Role of Families in Succession Decisions and Performance." *The Quarterly Journal of Economics* 122, no. 2, pp. 647–91.

Bettinelli, C. 2011. "Boards of Directors in Family Firms: An Exploratory Study of Structure and Group Process." *Family Business Review* 24, no. 2, pp. 151–69.

Bianco, M., A. Ciavarella, and R. Signoretti. 2015. "Women on Corporate Boards in Italy: The Role of Family Connections." *Corporate Governance: An International Review* 23, no. 2, pp. 129–44.

Black, B., and W. Kim. 2012. "The Effect of Board Structure on Firm Value: A Multiple Identification Strategies Approach Using Korean Data." *Journal of Financial Economics* 104, no. 1, pp. 203–26.

Bloom, N., and J. Van Reenen. 2007. "Measuring and Explaining Management Practices Across Firms and Countries." *The Quarterly Journal of Economics* 122, no. 4, pp. 1351–408.

BMI Research. 2018. Report Mexico country risk report Q1, Q4.

Brookfield, J. 2010. "The Network Structure of Big Business in Taiwan." *Asia Pacific Journal of Management* 27, no. 2, pp. 257–79.

Burkart, M., D. Gromb, and F. Panunzi. 1997. "Large Shareholders, Monitoring, and the Value of the Firm." *The Quarterly Journal of Economics* 112, no. 3, pp. 693–728.

Burkart, M., F. Panunzi, and A. Shleifer. 2003. "Family Firms." *The Journal of Finance* 58, no. 5, pp. 2167–2201.

Cárdenas, J. 2014. *El poder económico mundial: Análisis de redes de" interlocking directorates" y variedades de capitalismo*. Vol. 280. CIS-Centro de Investigaciones Sociológicas.

Cárdenas, J. 2016. "Why Do Corporate Elites Form Cohesive Networks in Some Countries, and Do not in Others? Cross-national Analysis of Corporate Elite Networks in Latin America." *International Sociology* 31, no. 3, pp. 341–63.

Casar, M.A. 2016. "Mexico: Anatomía de la Corrupción. IMCO. CIDE." 2ª edición. http://imco.org.mx/wp-content/uploads/2016/10/2016-Anatomia_Corrupcion_2-Documento.pdf.

Carpenter, M.A., and J.D. Westphal. 2001. "The Strategic Context of External Network Ties: Examining the Impact of Director Appointments on Board Involvement in Strategic Decision Making." *Academy of Management Journal* 44, no. 4, pp. 639–60.

Carter, D.A., B.J. Simkins, and W.G. Simpson. 2003. "Corporate Governance, Board Diversity, and Firm Value." *Financial Review* 38, no. 1, pp. 33–53.

Castro, S.M., C.J. Brown, and A. Báez-Díaz. 2009. Prácticas de gobierno corporativo en América Latina. *Academia. Revista latinoamericana de administración* no. 43.

CFA Institute. 2018. The Corporate Governance of Listed Companies: A Manual for Investors. https://www.cfainstitute.org/en/advocacy/policy-positions/corporate-governance-of-listed-companies-3rd-edition

Chang, S.J., and J. Shim. 2015. "When Does Transitioning from Family to Professional Management Improve Firm Performance?" *Strategic Management Journal* 36, no. 9, pp. 1297–316.

Chong, A., and F. López-de-Silanes. 2007. "Overview: Corporate Governance in Latin America." In *Investor Protection and Corporate Governance: Firm-level Evidence across Latin America.* Washington, DC: World Bank, pp. 1–84.

Chong, A., J. Guillen, and F. Lopez-de-Silanes. 2009. "Corporate Governance Reform and Firm Value in Mexico: An Empirical Assessment." *Journal of Economic Policy Reform* 12, no. 3, pp. 163–88.

Chua, J.H., J.J. Chrisman, and P. Sharma. 1999. "Defining the Family Business by Behavior." *Entrepreneurship Theory and Practice* 23, no. 4, pp. 19–39.

COFECE (comisión federal de competencia). 2018. Estudio sobre el impacto que tiene el poder de mercado en el bienestar de los hogares.

CONSAR (comisión nacional del sistema de ahorro). 2017. http://www.consar.gob.mx/gobmx/Aplicativo/Limites_Inversion/

Crabtree, R.G., and E.G. Gomolka. 1991. Perceptual barriers to consultant utilization: an examination of why manufacturers don't use consultants and what consultants can do about it. *Proceedings of the 36th ICSB World Conference.* Viena.

Credit Suisse. 2017. "Corporate Longevity." https://research-doc.credit-suisse.com/docView?language=ENG&format=PDF&sourceid=em&document_id=1070991801&serialid=TqtAPA%2FTEBUW%2BgCJnJNtlkenIBO4nHiIyPL7Muuz0FI%3D.

Dahya, J., O. Dimitrov, and J.J. McConnell. 2008. "Dominant Shareholders, Corporate Boards, and Corporate Value: A Cross-Country Analysis." *Journal of Financial Economics* 87, no. 1, pp. 73–100.

Del Hierro, P., and G. Alarco Tosoni. 2010. "Growth and Concentration among the Leading Business Groups in Mexico." *CEPAL Review.*

Deloitte. 2013. Quinto Estudio anual de mejores prácticas en Gobierno Corporativo.

Deloitte. 2018. Sexto Estudio anual de mejores prácticas en Gobierno Corporativo.

De Kluyver, C.A. 2009. *A Primer on Corporate Governance*. New York, NY: Business Expert Press.

Deutsch, Y. 2005. "The Impact of Board Composition on Firms Critical Decisions: A Meta Analytic Review." *Journal of Management* 31, no. 3, pp. 424–44.

Doidge, C., G.A. Karolyi, K.V. Lins, D.P. Miller, and R.M. Stulz. 2009. "Private Benefits of Control, Ownership, and the Cross-listing Decision." *The Journal of Finance* 64, no. 1, pp. 425–66.

Dowell, G.W., M.B. Shackell, and N.V. Stuart. 2011. "Boards, CEOs, and Surviving a Financial Crisis: Evidence from the Internet Shakeout." *Strategic Management Journal* 32, no. 10, pp. 1025–45.

Doz, Y.L., and M. Kosonen. June 2007. *The New Deal at the Top*. Brighton, MA: Harvard Business Review, pp. 1–7.

Dunn, P. 2004. "The Impact on Insider Power on Fraudulent Financial Reporting." *Journal of Management* 30, no. 3, pp. 397–412.

El Economista. Noviembre 29, 2018. "AMLO será el presidente con el tercer salario más bajo de la región." https://www.eleconomista.com.mx/politica/AMLO-sera-el-presidente-con-el-tercer-salario-mas-bajo-de-la-region-20181129-0044.html.

El Financiero. Febrero 13, 2019. "Mas caro el remedio que la enfermedad." https://www.elfinanciero.com.mx/opinion/enrique-quintana/mas-caro-el-remedio-que-la-enfermedad.

Eminet, A., and Z. Guedri. 2010. "The Role of Nominating Committees and Director Reputation in Shaping the Labor Market for Directors: An Empirical Assessment." *Corporate Governance: An International Review* 18, no. 6, pp. 557–74.

Erhardt, N.L., J.D. Werbel, and C.B. Shrader. 2003. "Board of Director Diversity and Firm Financial Performance." *Corporate Governance: An International Review* 11, no. 2, pp. 102–11.

Expansión revista. 2015. "Las 500 empresas más importantes de Mexico." https://expansion.mx/rankings/2018/07/12/las-500-empresas-mas-importantes-de-mexico-de-expansion-2015.

EY. 2015. "EY Center for Board Matters."

EY-ICSA. 2016. "The Nomination Committee: Coming out of the Shadows."

Faccio, M., M.T. Marchica, and R. Mura. 2016. "CEO Gender, Corporate Risk-taking, and the Efficiency of Capital Allocation." *Journal of Corporate Finance* 39, pp. 193–209.

Fainshmidt, S., W.Q. Judge, R.V. Aguilera, and A. Smith. 2018. "Varieties of Institutional Systems: A Contextual Taxonomy of Understudied Countries." *Journal of World Business* 53, no. 3, pp. 307–322.

Fama, E.F., and M.C. Jensen. 1983. "Agency Problems and Residual Claims." *Journal of Law and Economics* 26, no. 2, pp. 327–49.

Farinós Viñas, J.E., C.J. García Martin, B. Herrero Piqueras, and A.M. Ibáñez Escribano. 2016. "Revolving Doors: Are they Valued in the Spanish Stock Market?" *Academia Revista Latinoamericana de Administración* 29, no. 2, pp. 147–64.

Filatotchev, I., Y.C. Lien, & J. Piesse. 2005. "Corporate Governance and Performance in Publicly Listed, Family-Controlled Firms: Evidence from Taiwan." *Asia Pacific Journal of Management* 22, no. 3, pp. 257–83.

Financial Times. July 29th, 2019. "Lopez Obrador takes on Mexico's institutions" https://www.ft.com/content/69bf2628-b1e1-11e9-bec9-fdcab53d6959

Finkelstein, S., and D.C. Hambrick. 1990. "Top Management Team Tenure and Organizational Outcomes: The Moderating Role of Managerial Discretion." *Administrative Science Quarterly* 35, no. 3, pp. 484–503.

Finkelstein, S., D. Hambrick, and A. Canella. 2008. *Strategic Leadership: Theory and Research on Executives, Top Management Teams and Boards.* Oxford, England: Oxford University Press.

Forbes, D.P., and F.J. Milliken. 1999. "Cognition and Corporate Governance: Understanding Boards of Directors as Strategic Decision-making Groups." *Academy of Management Review* 24, pp. 489–505.

Franco A. 2015. *The Unbearable Cost of Distrust.* Washington, DC: Wilson Center.

Fredrickson, J., D. Hambrick, and S. Baumrin. 1988. "A Model of CEO Dismissal." *Academy of Management Journal* 13, pp. 255–70.

García-Sánchez, I.M. 2010. "The Effectiveness of Corporate Governance: Board Structure and Business Technical Efficiency in Spain." *Central European Journal of Operations Research* 18, no. 3, pp. 311–39.

Gedajlovic, E., M. Carney, J.J. Chrisman, & F.W. Kellermanns. 2012. "The Adolescence of Family Firm Research: Taking Stock and Planning for the Future." *Journal of Management* 38, no. 4, pp. 1010–37.

Goel, S., W. Voordeckers, A. Van Gils, and J. van den Heuvel. 2013. "CEO's Empathy and Salience of Socioemotional Wealth in Family SMEs–The Moderating Role of External Directors." *Entrepreneurship & Regional Development* 25, no. 3–4, pp. 111–34.

Goll, I., N. Brown Johnson, and A.A. Rasheed. 2007. "Knowledge Capability, Strategic Change, and Firm Performance: The Moderating Role of the Environment." *Management Decision* 45, no. 2, pp. 161–79.

Golden, B.R., and E.J. Zajac. 2001. "When will Boards Influence Strategy? Inclination × Power = Strategic Change." *Strategic Management Journal* 22, pp. 1087–111.

Gomez-Mejia, L.R., M. Nunez-Nickel, and I. Gutierrez. 2001. "The Role of Family Ties in Agency Contracts." *Academy of Management Journal* 44, no. 1, pp. 81–95.

Gómez-Mejía, L.R., K.T. Haynes, M. Núñez-Nickel, K.J. Jacobson, and J. Moyano-Fuentes. 2007. "Socioemotional Wealth and Business Risks in Family-controlled Firms: Evidence from Spanish Olive Oil Mills." *Administrative Science Quarterly* 52, no. 1, pp. 106–137.

Gomez-Mejia, L., P. Berrone, and M. Franco-Santos. 2010. *Strategic Compensation and Performance*. New York, NY: ME Sharpe.

Gomez-Mejia, L.R., C. Cruz, P. Berrone, and J. De Castro. 2011. "The Bind that Ties: Socioemotional Wealth Preservation in Family Firms." *Academy of Management Annals* 5, no. 1, pp. 653–707.

González, J.S., and E. García-Meca. 2014. "Does Corporate Governance Influence Earnings Management in Latin American markets?" *Journal of Business Ethics* 121, no. 3, pp. 419–40.

González Ferrero, M., A. Guzmán Vásquez, C. Pombo Bejarano, and M.A. Trujillo Dávila. 2010. "Empresas familiares: revisión de la literatura desde una perspectiva de agencia." *Cuadernos de Administración* 23, no. 40.

González, M., A. Guzmán, C. Pombo, and M.A. Trujillo. 2012. "Family Firms and Financial Performance: The Cost of Growing." *Emerging Markets Review* 13, no. 4, pp. 626–49.

González, M., A. Guzmán, C. Pombo, and M.A. Trujillo. 2015. "The Role of Family Involvement on CEO Turnover: Evidence from Colombian Family Firms." *Corporate Governance: An International Review* 23, no. 3, pp. 266–84.

Granovetter, M. 1985. "Economic Action and Social Structure: The Problem of Embeddedness." *American Journal of Sociology* 91, no. 3, pp. 481–510.

Granovetter, M. 2005. "Business Groups and Social Organization." In *The Handbook of Economic Sociology*, ed. N.J. Smelser, and R. Swedberg. (2nd ed.). Princeton, NJ: Princeton University Press.

Guillen, M.F. 2000. "Business Groups in Emerging Economies: A Resource-based View." *Academy of Management Journal* 43, no. 3, pp. 362–80.

Haber, S., N. Maurer, and A. Razo. 2003. *The Politics of Property Rights: Political Instability, Credible Commitments, and Economic Growth in Mexico, 1876-1929*. Cambridge: Cambridge University Press.

Hacksoon, K., and L. Chanwoo. 2010. "Diversity, Outside Directors and Firm Valuation: Korean Evidence." *Journal of Business Research* 63, no. 3, pp. 284–91.

Hambrick, D, and A. Canella. 1993. "Relative Standing: A Framework for Understanding Departures of Acquired Executives." *Academy of Management Journal* 36, no. 4, pp. 733–62.

Hambrick, D.C., and P.A. Mason. 1984. "Upper Echelons: The Organization as a Reflection of its Top Managers." *Academy of Management Review* 9, no. 2, pp. 193–206.

Haunschild, P.R. 1993. "Interorganizational Imitation: The Impact of Interlocks on Corporate Acquisition Activity." *Administrative Science Quarterly* 38, pp. 564–92.

Hellman, J., G. Jones, and D. Kaufmann. 2000. "Seize the State, Seize the Day: State Capture, Corruption, and Influence in Transition Economies. Working paper no. 2444 (Washington, DC: World Bank Policy Research).

Henke, J.W., Jr., 1986. "Involving the Board of Directors in Strategic Planning." *Journal of Business Strategy* 7, no. 2, pp. 87–95.

Heritage Foundation. 2018. "Index of Economic Freedom." https://www.heritage.org/index/country/mexico.

Herrmann, P., and D.K. Datta. 2002. "CEO Successor Characteristics and the Choice of Foreign Market Entry Mode: An Empirical Study." *Journal of International Business Studies* 33, no. 3, pp. 551–69.

Hillman, A.J., C. Shropshire, and A.A. Cannella, Jr. 2007. "Organizational Predictors of Women on Corporate Boards." *Academy of Management Journal* 50, no. 4, pp. 941–52.

INEGI. 2015. "Población." https://www.inegi.org.mx/temas/estructura/

Jehn, K.A. 1995. "A Multimethod Examination of the Benefits and Detriments of Intragroup Conflict." *Administrative Science Quarterly* 40, no. 2, pp. 256–82.

Jehn, K., G. Northcarft, and M. Neale. 1997. "Opening Pandora's Box: A Field Study of Diversity, Conflict and Performance in Work Groups." Working paper (Philadelphia, PA: Wharton School, University of Pennsylvania).

Jiang, Y., and M.W. Peng. 2011. "Principal-principal Conflicts During Crisis." *Asia Pacific Journal of Management* 28, no. 4, pp. 683–95.

Johnson, S., R. La Porta, F. Lopez-de-Silanes, and A. Shleifer. 2000. "Tunneling." *American Economic Review* 90, no. 2, pp. 22–27.

Judge, W., T. Douglas, and A. Kutan. 2008. "Institutional Antecedents of Corporate Governance Legitimacy." *Journal of Management* 34, pp. 765–86.

Katz, R. 1982. "The Effects of Group Longevity on Project Communication and Performance." *Administrative Science Quarterly* 27, pp. 81–104.

Kaufmann, D., A. Kray, and M. Mastruzzi, 2010. "The Worldwide Governance Indicators: Methodology and Analytical Issues". World Bank Policy Research Paper No. 5430 (Washington, DC: World Bank).

Khanna, T., and K. Palepu. 1999. "The Right Way to Restructure Conglomerates in Emerging Markets." *Harvard Business Review* 77, pp. 125–35.

Khanna, T., and J.W. Rivkin. 2001. "Estimating the Performance Effects of Business Groups in Emerging Markets." *Strategic Management Journal* 22, no. 1, pp. 45–74.

Khanna, T., and Y. Yafeh. 2007. "Business Groups in Emerging Markets: Paragons or Parasites?" *Journal of Economic Literature* 45, no. 2, pp. 331–72.

Khanna, P., C.D. Jones, and S. Boivie. 2014. "Director Human Capital, Information Processing Demands, and Board Effectiveness." *Journal of Management* 40, no. 2.

Kumar, P., and A. Zattoni. 2016. "Institutional Environment and Corporate Governance." *Corporate Governance: An International Review* 24, no. 2, pp. 82–84.

Lange, D., P.M. Lee, and Y. Dai. 2010. "Organizational Reputation: A Review." *Journal of Management* 37, no. 1, pp. 153–84.

La Porta, R., F. López-de-Silanes, and A. Shleifer. 1998. "Corporate Ownership around the World." Working paper no. 6625 (Cambridge, MA: National Bureau of Economic Research).

La Porta, R., F. Lopez-de-Silanes, A. Shleifer, and R. Vishny. 2000. "Investor Protection and Corporate Governance." *Journal of Financial Economics* 58, no. 1-2, pp. 3–27.

Leuz, C., and F. Oberholzer-Gee. 2006. "Political Relationships, Global Financing, and Corporate Transparency: Evidence from Indonesia." *Journal of Financial Economics* 81, pp. 411–39.

Leuz, C., K.V. Lins, and F.E. Warnock. 2009. "Do Foreigners Invest Less in Poorly Governed Firms?" *The Review of Financial Studies* 22, no. 8, pp. 3245–85.

Li, F., and S. Srinivasan. 2011. "Corporate Governance when Founders are Directors." *Journal of Financial Economics* 102, no. 2, pp. 454–69.

Lipton, M., and J.W. Lorsch. 1992. "A Modest Proposal for Improved Corporate Governance." *The Business Lawyer*, pp. 59–77.

Lynall, M.D., B.R. Golden, and A.J. Hillman. 2003. "Board composition from adolescence to maturity: A multitheoretic view." *Academy of Management Review* 28, no. 3, pp. 416–31.

Machuga, S., and K. Teitel. 2009. "Board of Director Characteristics and Earnings Quality Surrounding Implementation of a Corporate Governance Code in Mexico." *Journal of International Accounting, Auditing and Taxation* 18, no. 1, pp. 1–13.

Maurer, N., and T. Sharma. 2001. "Enforcing Property Rights through Reputation: Mexico's Early Industrialization, 1878–1913." *The Journal of Economic History* 61, no. 4, pp. 950–73.

Mehrotra, V., R. Morck, J. Shim, and Y. Wiwattanakantang. 2013. "Adoptive Expectations: Rising Sons in Japanese Family Firms." *Journal of Financial Economics* 108, no. 3, pp. 840–54.

Miller, D., I. Le Breton-Miller, R.H. Lester, and A.A. Cannella, Jr. 2007. "Are Family Firms really Superior Performers?" *Journal of Corporate Finance* 13, no. 5, pp. 829–58.

Millikens, F.J., and L.L. Martins. 1996. "Searching for Common Threads: Understanding the Multiple Effects of Diversity in Organizational Groups." *Academy of Management Review* 21, no. 2, pp. 402–33.

Minichilli, A., J. Gabrielsson, and M. Huse. 2007. "Board Evaluations: Making a Fit between the Purpose and the System." *Corporate Governance: An International Review* 15, no. 4, pp. 609–22.

Mizruchi, M.S. 1996. "What Do Interlocks Do? An Analysis, Critique, and Assessment of Research on Interlocking Directorates." *Annual Review of Sociology* 22, no. 1, pp. 271–98.

Monks, R., and N. Minow (eds.). 1995. *Corporate Governance*. Cambridge, MA: Blackwell Business.

Monks, R. A. G., & Minow, N. 2008. *Corporate governance*. West Sussex, UK: John Wiley

Musacchio, A., and I. Read. 2007. "Bankers, Industrialists, and their Cliques: Elite Networks in Mexico and Brazil during Early Industrialization." *Enterprise & Society* 8, no. 4, pp. 842–80.

Mutlu, C. C., Van Essen, M., Peng, M. W., Saleh, S. F., & Duran, P. (2018). Corporate Governance in China: A Meta-Analysis. *Journal of Management Studies*, 55(6), 943–979.

Neckebrouck, J., W. Schulze, and T. Zellweger. 2018. "Are Family Firms Good Employers?" *Academy of Management Journal* 61, no. 2, pp. 553–85.

Nemeth, C.J. 1992. "Minority Dissent as a Stimulant to Group Performance." In *Group Process and Productivity*, eds. S. Worchel, W. Wood and J.A. Simpson. Newbury Park, CA: Sage, pp. 95–111.

Newell, R., and G. Wilson. 2002. "A Premium for Good Governance." *McKinsey Quarterly* 3, no. 2, pp. 20–23.

North, D.C.1990. *Institutions, Institutional Change and Economic Performance*. New York, NY: Cambridge University Press.

OECD. 2018. Board Evaluation: Overview of International Practices.

Palia, D., S.A. Ravid, and C.J. Wang. 2008. "Founders Versus Nonfounders in Large Companies: Financial Incentives and the Call for Regulation." *Journal of Regulatory Economics* 33, no. 1, pp. 55–86.

Pelled, L.H., K.M. Eisenhardt, and K.R. Xin. 1999. "Exploring the Black Box: An Analysis of Work Group Diversity, Conflict and Performance." *Administrative Science Quarterly* 44, pp. 1–28.

Peng, M.W., and Y. Jiang 2010. "Institutions behind Family Ownership and Control in Large Firms." *Journal of Management Studies* 47, no. 2, pp. 253–73.

Pérez-González, F. 2006. "Inherited Control and Firm Performance." *American Economic Review* 96, no. 5, pp. 1559–88.

Pew Research Center. 2017. "How the US Hispanic Population is Changing." http://www.pewresearch.org/fact-tank/2017/09/18/how-the-u-s-hispanic-population-is-changing/.

PricewaterhouseCoopers. 2018. "Anticorrupción." https://www.pwc.com/mx/es/servicios-forenses/anticorrupcion.html.

PricewaterhouseCoopers. 2015. "Tercera Encuesta de Gobierno Corporativo en México: Entorno, tendencias y oportunidades." https://es.scribd.com/document/362295537/3era-Encuesta-Gobierno-Corporativo-2015-Noviembre.

Rhode, D., and A.K. Packel. 2014. "Diversity on Corporate Boards: How much Difference does Difference Make?" *Delaware Journal of Corporate Law* 39, no. 2, pp. 377–426.

Rindova, V.P., I.O. Williamson, A.P. Petkova, and J.M. Sever. 2005. "Being Good or Being Known: An Empirical Examination of the Dimensions, Antecedents, and Consequences of Organizational Reputation." *Academy of Management Journal* 48, no. 6, pp. 1033–1049.

Rivas, J.L. (2012a). "Diversity & Internationalization: The Case of Boards and TMT's." *International Business Review* 21, no. 1, pp. 1–12.

Rivas, J.L. (2012b). "Board versus TMT International Experience: A Study of their Joint Effects." *Cross Cultural Management: An International Journal* 19, no. 4, pp. 546–62.

Rivas, J.L., and J. Rubio. 2017. "Institutions and Corporate Governance Legitimacy: A Cross Country Study." *Academy of Management Proceedings* 2017, no. 1.

Rivas, J.L., and M. Adamuz. 2017. "Institutions and IPO Activity: A Multi Country Study." Working paper

Rivas, J.L. 2018. "Large Firms in Mexico: An Exploratory Study." Working paper.

Rivas, J.L., and J. Villamil. 2018. "Board Independence in Latin America—A Policy Perspective." Working paper.

Salas-Porras, A. (2006a). "Fuerzas centrípetas y centrífugas en la red corporativa mexicana (1981-2001)." *Revista mexicana de sociología* 68, no. 2, pp. 331–75.

Salas-Porras, A. (2006b). Los grupos mexicanos y coreanos ante el desmantelamiento del Estado. In *documento presentado en el 52º Congreso Internacional de Americanistas (Sevilla, España, 17 al 21 de julio de 2006). (2006b), "Fuerzas centrípetas y centrífugas en red corporativa mexicana (1981-2001)", Revista mexicana de sociología* (Vol. 68, No. 2).

San Martin-Reyna, J.M., and J.A. Duran-Encalada. 2012. "The Relationship among Family Business, Corporate Governance and Firm Performance: Evidence from the Mexican Stock Exchange." *Journal of Family Business Strategy* 3, no. 2, pp. 106–117.

Scott, J. 1991. "Networks of Corporate Power: A Comparative Assessment." *Annual Review of Sociology* 17, no. 1, pp. 181–203.

Scott, W.R. 1995. *Institutions and Organizations (Foundations for Organizational Science)*. London: A Sage Publication Series.

Shen, W., and A. Cannella. 2002. "Revisiting the Performance Consequences of CEO Succession: The Impacts of Successor Type, Post Succession Senior Executive Turnover, and Departing CEO Tenure." *Academy of Management Journal* 45, no. 4, pp. 717–33.

Shimizu, K. 2007. "Prospect Theory, Behavioral Theory and Threat Rigidity Thesis: Combinative Effects on Organizational Divestiture Decisions of a Formerly Acquired Unit." *Academy of Management Journal* 50, no. 6, pp. 1495–514.

Siegel, J. 2007. "Contingent Political Capital and International Alliances: Evidence from South Korea." *Administrative Science Quarterly* 52, no. 4, pp. 621–66.

Silvers, R.N., and P.T. Elgers. 2015. "The Valuation Impact of SEC Enforcement Actions on Non-Target Non-US Firms." http://dx.doi.org/10.2139/ssrn.1738576.

Spencer Stuart. 2017. "US Board Index." https://www.spencerstuart.com/~/media/ssbi2017/ssbi_2017_final.pdf.

Sraer, D., and D. Thesmar. 2007. "Performance and Behavior of Family Firms: Evidence from the French Stock Market." *Journal of the European Economic Association* 5, no. 4, pp. 709–51.

Strachan, H. 1979. "Nicaragua's Grupos Economicos: Scope and Operations." *Entrepreneurs in Cultural Context*, pp. 243–76.

The Economist. July 21, 2018. "Bello: A Misshapen Economy." https://www.economist.com/the-americas/2018/07/19/why-mexico-has-not-become-more-prosperous-and-how-it-could, (accessed October 7, 2018).

Thomsen, S., and T. Pedersen. 2000. "Ownership Structure and Economic Performance in the Largest European Companies." *Strategic Management Journal* 21, no. 689-705.

Villalonga, B., and R. Amit. 2008. "Family Control of Firms and Industries." Working Paper (Boston, MA: Harvard Business School).

Walsh, J.P. 1988. "Selectivity and Selective Perception: An Investigation of Managers' Belief Structures and Information Processing." *Academy of Management Journal* 31, no. 4, pp. 873–96.

Wang, D. 2006. "Founding Family Ownership and Earnings Quality." *Journal of Accounting Research* 44, no. 3, pp. 619–56.

Wang, C.L., and H.F. Chung. 2013. "The Moderating Role of Managerial Ties in Market Orientation and Innovation: An Asian Perspective." *Journal of Business Research* 66, no. 12, pp. 2431–37.

Wiersema, M.F., and K.A. Bantel. 1992. "Top Management Team Demography and Corporate Strategic Change." *Academy of Management Journal* 35, no. 1, pp. 91–121.

World Competitiveness Yearbook Data. 2004-2014. IMD. Geneva.

World Bank Group. 2016. *The Little Data*. Washington, DC: World Bank Publications.

You, J., and G. Du. 2012. "Are Political Connections a Blessing or a Curse? Evidence from CEO Turnover in China." *Corporate Governance: An International Review* 20, no. 2, pp. 179–94.

Young M.N., M.W. Peng, D. Ahlstrom, and G.D. Bruton. 2002. "Governing the Corporation in Emerging Economies: A Principal-Principal Perspective." In *Academy of Management Proceedings*. Vol. 2002, no. 1. Briarcliff Manor, NY: Academy of Management, pp. E1-E6.

Young, M.N., M.W. Peng, D. Ahlstrom, G.D. Bruton, and Y. Jiang. 2008. "Corporate Governance in Emerging Economies: A Review of the Principal–Principal Perspective." *Journal of Management Studies* 45, no. 1, pp. 196–220.

About the Author

Jose Luis Rivas is an associate professor at ITAM. He has held different positions at Inverlat Securities and Grupo ADO, where he was a board member for 8 years.

He holds a PhD in management from IE Business School and an MBA from Northwestern. His research interests focus on boards of directors, top management teams, and initial public offerings. He has published articles in journals such as *Journal of Management Studies and International Business Review*.

Jose also serves as editorial board member for *Corporate Governance: An International Review* and was designated as the country expert for Mexico at the International Corporate Governance Society.

Index

OTHER TITLES IN THE CORPORATE GOVERNANCE COLLECTION

John A. Pearce II and Kenneth A. Merchant, University of Southern California, *Editors*

- *A Primer on Corporate Governance: China* by Jean Jinghan Chen
- *Managerial Forensics* by J. Mark Munoz and Diana Heeb Bivona
- *A Primer on Corporate Governance:* Turkey by Sibel Yamak and Bengi Ertuna
- *A Primer on Corporate Governance:* Italy by Andrea Melis and Alessandro Zattoni

Announcing the Business Expert Press Digital Library

Concise e-books business students need for classroom and research

This book can also be purchased in an e-book collection by your library as

- a one-time purchase,
- that is owned forever,
- allows for simultaneous readers,
- has no restrictions on printing, and
- can be downloaded as PDFs from within the library community.

Our digital library collections are a great solution to beat the rising cost of textbooks. E-books can be loaded into their course management systems or onto students' e-book readers.

The **Business Expert Press** digital libraries are very affordable, with no obligation to buy in future years. For more information, please visit **www.businessexpertpress.com/librarians**. To set up a trial in the United States, please email **sales@businessexpertpress.com**.

www.ingramcontent.com/pod-product-compliance
Lightning Source LLC
Chambersburg PA
CBHW061334220326
41599CB00026B/5177

9781631575815